CW00362194

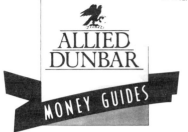

PLANNING YOUR
PENSION

PLANNING YOUR PENSION

Tony Reardon

© Allied Dunbar Financial Services Limited 1988

ISBN 0–85121–371–5

Published by

Longman Professional and Business Communications Division
Longman Group UK Limited
21–27 Lamb's Conduit Street, London WC1N 3NJ

Associated Offices

Australia   Longman Professional Publishing (Pty) Limited
130 Phillip Street, Sydney, NSW 2000

Hong Kong   Longman Group (Far East) Limited
Cornwall House, 18th Floor, Taikoo Trading Estate,
Tong Chong Street, Quarry Bay

Malaysia   Longman Malaysia Sdn Bhd
No 3 Jalan Kilang A, Off Jalan Penchala,
Petaling Jaya, Selangor, Malysia

Singapore   Longman Singapore Publishers (Pte) Ltd
25 First Lok Yang Road, Singapore 2262

USA   Longman Group (USA) Inc
500 North Dearborn Street, Chicago, Illinois 60610

The examples in this book are based on typical pension contracts and, unless it is
stated to the contrary, future investment return is assumed to be 13% per annum
and annuities are based on an underlying interest rate of 10% per annum.

The book is based on Allied Dunbar Assurance's understanding of the law and
current Inland Revenue practice and incorporates the changes proposed in the
March 1988 Budget. There is no guarantee that these proposals will become law
and, in view of the fact that Inland Revenue practice can change from time to time,
it is recommended that you discuss any alteration to your pension arrangements with
your usual financial adviser. You will appreciate that Allied Dunbar can accept no
responsibility for any financial loss resulting from action taken (or not taken) as a
result of reading this book.

A CIP catalogue record for this book is available from the British Library.

Printed in Great Britain by Biddles Ltd, Guildford, Surrey.

Tony Reardon

Tony Reardon is the Division Director of Allied Dunbar
Assurance's Pensions Marketing Department where he is
involved in the design of new pension products and
monitoring changes in pensions legislation – of which there
have been far too many recently!

His job also consists of talking to groups of people, for
example intermediates, accountants, solicitors about the
tax-efficient opportunities afforded by pension schemes.

He is also the author of the Allied Dunbar Pensions Guide.

At-a-glance pension planner

Generally speaking it is going to be worth reading the first three chapters of this book, but then you may wish to be selective.

Happy with your company pension?
- You can now leave your company scheme and take out your own personal pension
- You can top up your pension either by paying more to your company scheme or by taking out your own plan
- If you leave SERPS at the same time, the DHSS will contribute to your pension

See Chapters 3, 4, 6, 8 & 9

Want to retire early?
- The new personal pension plans let you retire at any time between 50 and 75

See Chapters 6 & 12

Relying on the State?
- The self-employed get only the old age pension
- SERPS is being drastically reduced

See Chapters 3, 4 & 6

Running your own company?
- Use an executive plan to shelter your profits
- How you can personalise company wealth

See Chapters 6, 13 & 14

Thinking of changing jobs?
- New benefits for those leaving their existing scheme
- No need to join the pension scheme of your new employer

See Chapters 6, 8 & 10

Are you in SERPS?
- You can now leave SERPS and take out your own pension and the DHSS will pay for it
- For the six years you get an incentive to take out a personal pension

See Chapters 3, 4, 6, 8 & 9

Are you self-employed?
- New rules on personal pension plans from 1 July 1988
- A chance to take out a retirement annuity plan before 30 June 1988

See Chapters 5 & 6

Looking for a mortgage?
- A pension related mortgage can be a very tax efficient way of buying your home
- You can now use a company scheme to help you
- The lifetime loan option can mean continuing tax efficiency

See Chapters 10 & 6

Wanting to maximise tax relief?
- Life assurance with full tax relief
- Maximum tax-free lump sums permitted by Inland Revenue
- Paying contributions for previous years to obtain higher rates of relief

See Chapters 6, 14 & 15

Introduction

The topic of pensions can arouse varying emotions.

If you are young, pensions are boring: what possible interest will you have in a pension which starts in 40 years' time – at retirement – when you are 65? You are probably more interested in the present and your earnings now. In fact, pensions probably conjures up images of old age and you would probably much rather think about sport, fast cars, fashion, holidays.

If you have your own business you may think that pensions are unnecessary. After all, your business is successful now, and you expect that you will be able to sell it in the future for a sum which will provide you with an income. Or perhaps you think that you will never retire. Your family has been in business for generations and you expect to pass it on to your children. You will continue to work and receive an income from the business.

Perhaps you are married, with children, in your thirties or forties. You have a nagging feeling that you should have a pension as your employer may not provide one. Despite this you have other priorities and you think that you can put off any serious thoughts of pension until you are closer to retirement.

If you are a pensioner you will probably have a completely different view: you are probably worried about the inadequacy of your pension. All you have is a State Pension and some savings which you have to dip into from time to time to top up your income. Whatever capital you had when you retired is being eroded as years go by.

Even if you have avoided the subject in the past you will find it difficult to do so in 1988. The Government has thought about pensions in a new light: the results of its thinking, amid a welter of Green Papers, White Papers, Bills, Acts and Regulations are that State pensions, already inadequate, will be lower in the future. The Government is also encouraging people to take out personal pensions and is improving the options of occupational scheme members. Whatever your age you too should think about pensions in a new light.

The list of major changes is quite extensive:

- The benefits to be provided by the State Earnings Related Pension Scheme (SERPS) are to be reduced.
- Employees are being encouraged to withdraw from SERPS and take out one of the new personal pension plans.
- The Government will, in certain circumstances, contribute to your personal pension.
- Personal pensions for the self-employed are to be changed from 1 July 1988.
- Employees will have the right to withdraw from their company scheme or top up the benefits with their own personal arrangements.

We are retiring younger and living longer. It is pointless to expect the State to finance this – we look to the Government only to protect our old age and to help us preserve a certain basic standard of living. We cannot expect anyone but ourselves to pay the cost of a longer 'holiday' or to enable us to live in the way to which we have become accustomed.

The decision which you make in 1988 on pensions will probably have a major affect on your future standard of living, and that of your family. In many cases, you will need to look for financial advice to help you in making these decisions, but this book will help you to identify which decisions have to be made.

The table overleaf will help you decide which chapters of this book are most relevant to your circumstances. However, faced with many Government changes to pensions legislation and more choices being opened up to you, it is likely that much of this book will provide some useful insight into the rapidly evolving pensions scene which you can use to your financial planning advantage.

Invest a day in your future – read this book.

Contents

1 What is the point of a pension?

In 1908, Lloyd George gave retired men an old age pension of 5/ – a week. That represented about 20% of the national average wage at the time. For a single person today, nothing much has changed – it is still about 20%.

Some things *have* changed:

- In 1908, the life expectancy for a man was just under 49 years; today, it is over 70.
- Today, we have the income related benefit provided by SERPS to look forward to, although the changes the Government is introducing will mean that very few will benefit from the maximum level of pension it was originally intended to provide.
- More people belong to company pension schemes, but around 10,000,000 people still don't.

The point of a pension is to ensure that your income continues in the future. Most people are terrified at the thought that their income might stop, for example through redundancy, especially as in the recent past there has been a dramatic increase in unemployment. In fact, that is what happens at retirement: your earned income stops because you have left work.

The point of a pension, therefore, is to give up some of your earned income now and put it on one side until you retire. The accumulated money is then used to provide you with an income for the rest of your life.

Another way of looking at a pension is to regard it as 'deferred pay'. Fortunately, many employers provide pensions for employees. Many do not and all their employees will have to rely on will be State pensions.

Saving for the future

If you are to ensure that your income does continue in retirement then you will have to set aside money now. There are various ways of doing this but in order to encourage people to build up a source of income for when they retire, successive governments have given generous tax reliefs to those who are prepared to give up their income now and to save through pension plans of some description.

The self-employed

If you are self-employed there is no question of an employer providing you with a pension in retirement. There is no employer as such: you are the employer and employee combined. You, therefore, have the sole responsibility of ensuring that when you retire from your business you are able to enjoy a comfortable standard of living. Many self-employed people forget to do this as they are so busy running their businesses. In fact, the business is running them and they can never afford to retire.

If you are self-employed the pension plan that you can provide for yourself is very similar to pensions for employed people to the extent that the generous tax reliefs are very similar. The structure of self-employed pension plans, however, is different as you will find out later on in this book: Chapter 5 deals specifically with retirement benefits for the self-employed.

Occupational schemes

If you are a member of an occupational scheme, you may
know little of the benefits provided under it. You may be
merely aware that you are a member of the scheme but
because the employer has taken on the responsibility of
providing you with pension benefits you have never concerned
yourself with the responsibility of considering whether those
benefits will be adequate. Even if you are a member of a
contributory scheme where deductions are made from your
pay each month it is possible that you have never really
investigated the adequacy of the benefits. Employers now
have to provide much more information than in the past, but
it may still be a daunting task to find out what all the jargon
means.

You will find more details about the kind of benefits your
scheme might provide in Chapter 8.

Additional Voluntary Contributions

If you are a member of an occupational scheme and have
taken the time to investigate its benefits you have probably
realised that they are inadequate. Very few occupational
schemes provide anything like the maximum benefits
permitted by the Inland Revenue. Most employers quite
simply could not afford to provide these maximum benefits.
However, you can 'top up' the occupational scheme benefits
by paying Additional Voluntary Contributions (AVCs). The
generous tax reliefs mentioned in previous paragraphs also
apply to AVC schemes which are described in more detail
in Chapter 9.

The State

The 'point of a pension' as far as governments are concerned has varied during the years. Initially, State benefits were means tested and were designed to provide a level of subsistence income in retirement. But this has proved to be a moving target and there have been numerous changes in the way the State has seen its responsibility. The State Earnings Related Pension Scheme (SERPS), for example, was introduced in 1978, and was designed to provide maximum benefits for those retiring in 1998. After only 10 years of its existence this scheme is being amended considerably and these amendments will mean reductions in State pensions.

Inevitably, further changes will be made by governments in the future: these amendments may increase State pensions or they may reduce State pensions – who knows? Whatever happens it would be very risky to expect the State to provide anything more than the bare minimum as far as pension requirements are concerned. It is probably better to work on the basis that any income in retirement either comes from your own resources, your employer's resources or a combination of the two and that any State benefits paid in the future will be a bonus. That way you will not be disappointed.

Chapter 3 has more details on State pensions.

The opportunities

A pension plan is a virtually unbeatable investment. You obtain tax relief on the contributions which you pay, and the funds in which your contributions are invested grow free of UK income and capital taxes. If you die, the benefits will be returned to your dependants free of inheritance tax. On retirement generally a portion of the fund may be taken in cash completely tax-free with the remainder being used to provide you with an income for life. This income is also taxed in the same way as your income today is taxed.

The following chapters will cover the opportunities that this framework provides for ensuring that you build up a worthwhile income in retirement regardless of your status now.

The Government has already signalled that there is a limit to the amount it is prepared to provide, or is able to provide the pensioners of tomorrow. What is clear is that the State expects the individual to take far more interest in his future pension and that means making plans today.

2 The changing face of pensions

'The State pension will be adequate'.

It won't be. The State recognised long ago that it had a duty a provide a basic income for people who stopped working. But the State does not consider that it has an obligation to keep us in the standard of living that we have achieved while we have been working. That is up to us and we have to take advantage of the opportunities offered by successive governments in making it easier to prepare for the day we stop working.

Pension sources

When you retire your pension will probably come from a number of sources:

- the State,
- occupational pension schemes,
- personal pension plans.

The proportion of total pension that you will receive from each of these sources depends on a number of factors. For example, you may have been employed by a number of employers none of whom had an occupational scheme, in which case your sole income in retirement will come from the State. Or, perhaps for a few years, you will be employed and will join an occupational scheme, in which case you will be entitled to a pension from that scheme when you retire. If you are self-employed for part of your working life, then any pension provision will have come from a personal pension plan: indeed there will be an even greater need for you to take out a personal pension plan as State benefits have always been particularly low for the self-employed.

As a result of changes to pension legislation (mainly the Social Security Act 1986) you will find that in the future a much lower proportion of your pension in retirement will come from the State which means that a much higher proportion will have to come from other sources if you are not to experience a serious reduction in living standards in retirement.

The problem with State pensions – the ageing population

State pensions are provided on a 'pay as you go' basis. In other words today's pensioners are paid directly out of the income received by the State from the National Insurance Contributions and taxes paid by today's earners. This is in contrast to an occupational scheme set up by an employer or an individual personal pension plan, where contributions are paid into a fund and invested so that at the end of a period the accumulated sum is used to purchase a pension or an annuity.

According to the Green Paper, *Reform of Social Security* published in June 1985, the proportion of national income required to finance Social Security benefits (including pensions) during the last 40 years has more than doubled and in the last 15 years it has increased by more than half. One of the reasons for this is population changes. The number of elderly people has increased substantially in recent years and will begin to increase rapidly again at the start of the next century due to the higher number of births in the mid-1950s and 1960s. Also, it is to be hoped that people will live longer as a result of improvements in medical science. Overall,

there will be a substantially increased number of retired
people.

The estimated growth in the number of retired people is as
follows:

1985	—	9.3 million
1995	—	9.8 million
2005	—	10.0 million
2015	—	11.1 million
2025	—	12.3 million
2035	—	13.2 million

Source: Green Paper, *Reform of Social Security*

The number of pensioners is not a problem in itself. The real
problem is that there will be an insufficient number of people
working to pay the national insurance contributions and taxes
to finance pensions for those who have retired. In fact, the
number of contributors paying for pensions in the future will
be very similar to the number of contributors today. In
summary, the balance of the population is changing.

The following table shows the proportion of contributors to
pensioners in future years:

1985	—	2.3 contributors to each pensioner
1995	—	2.2 contributors to each pensioner
2005	—	2.2 contributors to each pensioner
2015	—	2.0 contributors to each pensioner
2025	—	1.8 contributors to each pensioner
2035	—	1.6 contributors to each pensioner

Source: Green Paper, *Reform of Social Security*

As a result of these changes in population, the Government
has concluded that the State Earnings Related Pension
Scheme cannot be maintained at its current level.
Consequently, State pensions for employees retiring in the
next century will be lower in order to reduce the amount of
Government expenditure. However, as well as reducing the

earnings related pension, the Government is encouraging us to contribute to our own personal pensions and is also encouraging more employers to set up occupational pension schemes for their employees.

Currently, only around one half of the working population (about 11 million) are members of occupational schemes. The Government is hoping to persuade everyone to take far more interest in their future retirement plans. The opportunities for introducing occupational pension schemes and for topping up existing schemes are going to be widely publicised in the coming months and years.

Although the Government in future years will still be paying out retirement pensions, the individual is going to be expected to take on a growing part of the responsibility for providing for his own retirement. How much of that responsibility *you* are prepared to take on will depend on how much you value security or having a comfortable retirement. If you have been content to rely on the State for your retirement benefits, then you need to be very much aware that the Government intends reducing your future benefits. It might now be better to work on the basis that 'the State will not provide' and to start thinking more seriously about your own plans. If the State does provide a pension in the future (or if a future government increases pensions), it might be better to regard that as a bonus, rather than as a right.

'Pensions are for old people'.

Pensions may be paid when you're old – because that's when you need the money. But if you regard a pension as an income for when you're no longer working then it's clear that it's best to start planning when you're young.

Think what you would do if you were suddenly given 10 weeks holiday, the planning you would do – and the sudden question 'can we afford it?' Regard your retirement as being a 10 year holiday. Or perhaps longer. Are you planning for it? Could you afford it?

The State provides you with the following retirement pensions:

- the basic pension,
- the graduated pension,
- the earnings related pension.

These pensions are taxable and all become payable when you reach State retirement age (which is age 60 for a woman and age 65 for a man).

Basic pension

The basic pension, if you are single, amounts to £41.15 per week (£2,139.80 per annum) for the tax year which runs from 6 April 1988 to 5 April 1989. The basic pension is around 20% of national average earnings.

If you are married the pension is increased to £65.90 per week (£3,426.80 per annum).

To obtain the maximum basic pension you have to satisfy a number of conditions but generally you must have paid, or you must have been credited with, National Insurance contributions for about 90% of your working life. The basic pension used to be increased each year in line with the greater of prices and earnings (as measured by the Retail Prices Index and the National Average Earnings Index). Now it is only increased in line with prices and in recent years, prices have increased less quickly than earnings. One particular point of interest for the self-employed is that the old age pension is the only State pension that they can qualify for.

Graduated pensions

In 1961 the Government introduced the graduated pension scheme to supplement the basic pension: it operated from April 1961 until April 1975 and related benefits and contributions to earnings. The amount of graduated pension depends on the number of units credited to you which in turn depends on your graduated contributions paid between those dates. Currently, the graduated supplement amounts to a maximum of £5.39 per week (if you are a woman you get a pension of 5p for every £9 you have paid in graduated contributions: if you are a man you get 5p for every £7.50 you have paid in contributions).

State Earnings Related Pension Scheme

The State Earnings Related Pension Scheme (SERPS) is an additional State scheme open to employees only (ie, not the self-employed). Whether you are in SERPS currently depends on your employer and whether or not you are in a company scheme that provides you with a pension:

- If you are in a pension scheme then you *may not* be in SERPS. If you are *not* in SERPS then you are in 'contracted-out' employment. The decision not to be in SERPS is your employer's (up to 5 April 1988).
- If you are not in a company scheme, then you *will* be in SERPS – and your employer does not have the choice. This is known as 'contracted-in' employment.

The State Earnings Related Pension Scheme is based on the national insurance contributions you and your employer pay on your earnings between the lower earnings limit (currently £41 per week or £2,132 per annum) and the upper earnings limit (currently £305 per week or £15,860 per annum). The amount of your earnings which lies between these two figures is sometimes known as 'band earnings'.

SERPS – original level

SERPS when introduced in April 1978 was originally designed to provide a pension of one-quarter of band earnings if you retired in 1998 or later. In arriving at the level of 'earnings' the Government had originally intended to increase your actual earnings during your working lifetime in line with increases in national average earnings up to retirement and then pick the average of the best 20 years. One quarter (ie, 25%) of this notional average earnings figure would then be paid as the Earnings Related Pension.

EXAMPLE 1

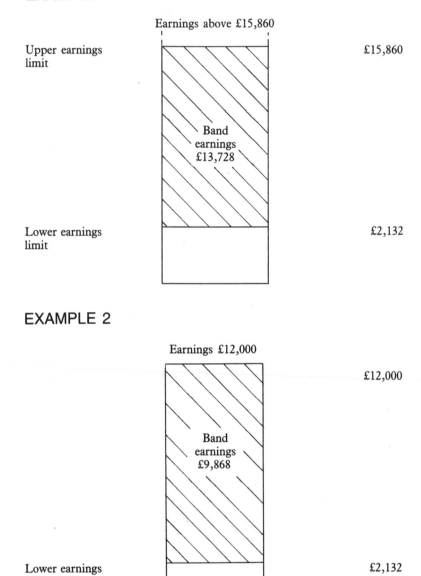

Earnings above £15,860

Upper earnings limit	£15,860
	Band earnings £13,728
Lower earnings limit	£2,132

EXAMPLE 2

Earnings £12,000

	£12,000
	Band earnings £9,868
Lower earnings limit	£2,132

In this way you could look forward to a lifetime pension of 25% of your average salary (increased in line with average earnings). Note – only 25%.

If you reach State retirement age before 6 April 1999 your pension will be 1 1/4% (or 1/80th) of the total notional earnings figures calculated as above for all the years you have been contributing to SERPS since 1978.

Reduced SERPS

However, if you reach State retirement age after 5 April 1999, SERPS will be reduced. The main changes to SERPS are:

- The current system of averaging the best 20 years earnings will no longer apply. Instead, earnings will be averaged over your whole working lifetime. The effect this will have on your pension depends on your earnings pattern but the following example will give you an indication of what might happen.

EXAMPLE

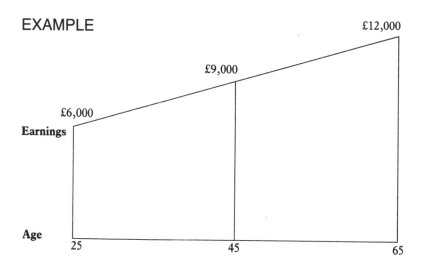

The above simplified example shows an individual's salary commencing at £6,000 per annum (age 25) rising to £9,000 by age 45 and £12,000 at State retirement age. It is assumed that the increases of £3,000 and £6,000 are *real* increases, ie, over and above inflation. Under the old basis SERPS pension would have been based on the average of the last 20 years earnings starting at £9,000 and ending at £12,000, ie, an average of £10,500 (assuming uniform increases).

- Under the new basis SERPS pension will be based on the average of the earnings for the whole period starting at £6,000 and ending at £12,000, giving an average of £9,000.
- If your earnings reach the upper earnings limit (currently £15,860) the impact of this new averaging process will have less effect and if your earnings reach the upper earnings limit early in life the impact will be small.
— The maximum benefits if you reach State retirement age in the tax year 2009/2010 or later will only be 20% of band earnings.
— The combination of these two changes can be significant.
— In the figures shown previously, calculating an average salary on the 20 best years produced an average of £10,500. 25% of this is £2,625.
— On the new basis the average is £9,000 of which 20% is £1,800.
— Expressed as a percentage of final salary, ie, income immediately before retirement the pension will fall from 22% to a mere 15%.
— If you retire between 1998 and 2010 the percentage will be on a sliding scale as follows:

Retirement year	Percentage
1999/2000	25
2000/2001	24½
2001/2002	24
2002/2003	23½
2003/2004	23
2004/2005	22½

2005/2006	22
2006/2007	21½
2007/2008	21
2008/2009	20½
2009/2010 or later	20

Old rules and new rules

If you reach SRA after 5 April 1999 your SERPS benefits will be based on your average band earnings over all the tax years since 1978/79 to the last complete tax year before you reach SRA. Your band earnings will be split into two parts:

1   The tax years 1978/79 to 1987/88.
2   The tax years from 1988/89.

Your total earnings for the first period are multipled by 25% and then divided by the number of years between 1978/79 and the last complete tax year before you reach SRA: this gives an average.

Your total earnings for the second period are multiplied by the reduced figure between 20–25% as set out in the above list, and divided by the same number of years to SRA. The results of the two calculations are added together to give the annual rate of SERPS.

EXAMPLE

If you retire on 1 December 2008 your pension will be calculated as follows:

$\frac{10}{30} \times 25\% \times$ (average of your earnings between 6 April 1978 and 5 April 1988)

plus

$\frac{20}{30} \times 20\frac{1}{2}\% \times$ (average of your earnings between 6 April 1988 and 5 April 2008)

The following table shows the pension (basic plus SERPS) which you could expect to receive from the State. For example, a single woman aged 45 currently earning £9,000 could expect to retire with a State pension of 42.2% of her final earnings, ie, £3,795 per annum in today's terms. A single man aged 55 earning £20,000 could expect to retire with a State pension of 28% of his final earnings, ie, £5,600 in today's terms.

Table 1

Single woman who will retire at age 60

Total earnings		£7,000	£9,000	£15,860	£20,000
Age	25	45.6	40.1	31.9	25.3
	35	45.8	40.4	32.2	25.5
	45	47.5	42.2	34.3	27.2
	55	44.0	38.4	29.9	23.7
	60	39.6	33.6	24.5	19.4

Single man who will retire at age 65

Total earnings		£7,000	£9,000	£15,860	£20,000
Age	25	45.5	40.1	31.8	25.2
	35	45.7	40.3	32.0	25.4
	45	46.2	40.9	32.7	25.9
	55	48.3	43.1	35.3	28.0
	60	44.0	38.4	29.9	23.7
	65	39.6	33.6	24.5	19.4

In the above examples it has been assumed that your earnings will increase in line with increases in national average earnings.

Widows

Currently, a SERPS dependant's pension is payable where the deceased leaves a widow over the age of 40 and/or dependent children. If the widow is aged between 40 and 50, the maximum pension is reduced. If there are no dependent children, but the widow is aged 50 or over she inherits the whole of the SERPS benefit (see Diagram 1). From the next century, the SERPS dependant's pension will only be payable where the deceased leaves a widow aged 45 or over and/or dependent children and the pension will be only one half of the SERPS benefit (see Diagram 2).

Some more facts about State pensions

Early retirement

You cannot receive a State pension before you reach age 60 for a woman or age 65 for a man. If, for example, you have been made redundant late in your working life, with little prospect of re-employment, you should be aware that a State pension will not be payable until State pension age.

Late retirement

You can defer your retirement beyond State pension age if you want to return to work or you can cancel your retirement and give up your pension temporarily. If you put off or cancel your retirement, your pension will be increased when you finally retire. However, you cannot defer your retirement beyond age 65 if you are a woman or age 70 if you are a man.

The earnings rule

If you are a woman under age 65 or a man under age 70 you can earn up to £75 a week before it affects your basic pension. The earnings rule does not affect any graduated pension or any SERPS pension.

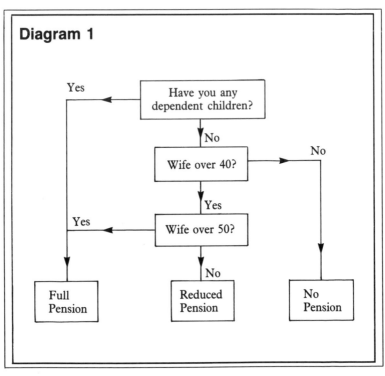

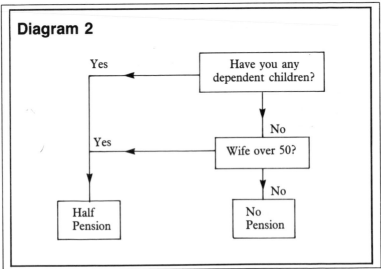

If your earnings are above £75 per week the amount of your basic pension is reduced by half of the first £4 per week of any excess and the whole of any excess above £4 per week.

Married women

If you are a married woman you can qualify for a pension as follows:

- if you paid enough National Insurance Contributions at the full rate you can get a basic pension in the same way as a man or a single woman, or
- you can receive a basic pension based on your husband's contributions if he is receiving his pension, you are over age 60 and you can be treated as having retired.

The pension that you receive will normally be the higher of these two pensions described above.

State pensions in general

This chapter has described briefly the various State benefits and the changes to SERPS for those retiring in the next century. Numerous leaflets are available from Department of Health and Social Security offices describing State benefits in detail. However, the overall message, for the prospective pensioner is that State pensions are extremely complicated and will probably have reduced significantly by the time retirement becomes a reality.

Contracting-out of SERPS

It is possible to be 'contracted-out' of SERPS. If you are contracted-out the State will not provide you with an earnings related pension (although you will not lose out on SERPS benefits altogether) but an equivalent amount will be provided by your employer under a contracted-out occupational pension scheme.

The only way, up to April 1988, in which your employer has been able to withdraw you from SERPS has been to provide, via a company pension scheme, benefits that are at least equal to the benefits provided by SERPS.

Moreover, the decision as to whether or not you are in SERPS has been your employer's. From 1 July 1988, *you* will be able to decide whether or not you are a member of SERPS and this is explained in the next chapter.

Forecast service

The DHSS are able to provide you with a forecast of your retirement benefits. All you have to do is obtain form NP38 from your local DHSS office, enter your name, address, date of birth, and National Insurance number on the form and return it to the office. The DHSS will then provide you with an estimate of your retirement benefits, and what they would be worth in today's terms. It is a very useful service which you should take advantage of regularly.

4 Personal pensions for employed persons – contracting-out

'Pensions are complicated'.

Pensions themselves are not complicated. The legislation surrounding pensions is extremely complicated – but that is a problem for the pension provider, the Inland Revenue and the DHSS.

A pension means giving up income now (and not paying tax on it) in return for having an income in retirement (which may be taxable then). For the individual, it's one of the simplest – and most tax-efficient – ways of saving there is.

Introduction of personal pension plans

From 1 July 1988 you will be able to take out a personal pension plan through a wide range of pension providers. As well as insurance companies and friendly societies, unit trusts, banks and building societies will also be able to offer you a personal pension plan. In fact, personal pension plans are not really new: they have been available to employed people who are not in a company pension scheme for many years in the guise of retirement annuity contracts.

Main features

The main features of a personal pension plan are as follows:

- Up to 17½% of your earnings may be paid into a plan, with higher limits for people over 50.
- You will not be liable to any income tax on any contributions that you pay into your personal pension plan.
- Contributions will be invested in a fund which itself grows absolutely free of all UK taxes on income and capital gains.
- Your contributions will be paid in a similar way to mortgage interest payments, ie, they will be paid net of basic rate income tax. If you are a higher rate taxpayer, you will get further tax relief through your tax assessment.
- At retirement (or earlier) the accumulated fund can be used to provide you with a pension and, if you wish, a tax free cash lump sum:
— You can start your pension at any time between the ages of 50 and 75 and you will not in fact have to retire before starting your pension.
— 25% of the fund built up can be taken as a cash lump sum completely free of tax (although this will reduce the amount of your retirement income).
— The pension will be paid to you for the rest of your life and will be taxed as earned income.
- Life assurance protection can be included in your retirement plan with full tax relief on contributions (the only way that employees can buy life assurance and get tax relief on the contributions).
- Your employer will be able to pay contributions into the plan on your behalf.
- You will be able to build in sickness protection to ensure that your contributions are maintained on your behalf if you are unable to work as a result of illness or injury.

Overall, a personal pension plan can be a very attractive and tax efficient way of building up funds for retirement. It will be *your* plan and may be taken with you from job to job.

If you are currently employed but not in an occupational pension scheme (and there are around 11 million people in this situation), then you are *currently* eligible for a retirement annuity contract. A retirement annuity contract provides very similar benefits to those provided by a personal pension plan but there are two important differences:

- You can start your pension at any time between the ages of 60 and 75 (and not 50 and 75 as you can under a personal pension plan).
- Approximately one-third of the fund built up can be taken as a cash lump sum completely free of tax (and not 25% which will be the position under a personal pension plan).

If you do not have an existing retirement annuity contract, then you can take one out provided you act before the 30 June 1988. From 1 July 1988, retirement annuity contracts will be replaced by personal pension plans.

Contracting-out through personal pension plans

The new pension legislation which becomes effective from 1 July 1988 is a direct result of the Government's conclusions on State pensions:

- The Government has concluded that the proposed level of SERPS benefits cannot be met in the future and so proposes to reduce the level of benefits payable from 1999 onwards.
- In addition, the Government is introducing the means for people to take out their own personal pension plans and will allow individuals to use these plans as the basis for

withdrawing from SERPS if they wish. The Government is also offering financial incentives to those people who withdraw from SERPS.

Consequently, if you take out a new personal pension plan from 1 July 1988 onwards you will be able to use it to contract-out of SERPS. Currently, you may only be contracted-out if you are a member of your employer's occupational scheme which is contracted-out and which provides a specific level of benefits based on final pay.

The Government will now allow *you* to make the decision to contract-out of SERPS as it is keen to encourage contracting-out. The number of persons contracted-out has not increased since the facility first became available in 1978 – in fact the numbers have reduced. In the past only employers had the choice to set up an occupational scheme and use it to contract-out of SERPS. From 1 July 1988 *you* will have the option. Naturally, you will sacrifice the SERPS benefits that you would have been entitled to but you will be able to build up your own pension plan because the DHSS pay part of your national insurance contributions directly into your personal pension plan.

Clearly, by giving up SERPS, you are giving up *some* benefits. What will be of importance, therefore, is to know what percentage of your income would have to be paid into an occupational scheme to provide equivalent benefits – known as a guaranteed minimum pension (GMP).

Table 2 shows the percentage of band earnings that would have to be paid into an occupational scheme to produce benefits equal to SERPS.

You will see that it depends on your age and sex. It is always more expensive for women (because they tend to retire earlier and live longer); it is always more expensive for older people because there is less time to build up a retirement fund.

Consequently, in deciding whether or not *you* should contract

Table 2: The cost of providing GMP

Age	Men	Women
16–19	2.2%	2.9%
20–24	2.2%	3.0%
25–29	2.4%	3.5%
30–34	2.8%	4.2%
35–39	3.4%	5.2%
40–44	4.3%	6.6%
45–49	5.4%	8.7%
50–54	7.1%	10.9%
55–59	9.0%	12.5%
60–64	10.5%	–

Source: Government Actuary's *Review of Certain Contracting-Out Terms* March 1987

out of SERPS, you should bear in mind exactly what you are giving up and how much it will cost you to replace it.

A reduction in National Insurance contributions

The National Insurance contributions payable at contracted-in rates are as follows:

Employee – 9% of earnings up to a maximum of £15,860 (ie, the upper limit of 'band earnings')
Employer – 10.45% of earnings with no upper limit

(However, you pay lower National Insurance contributions if your earnings are below £5,460 per annum and your employer will pay a lower rate if your earnings are below £8,060 per annum.)

If you are contracted-out of SERPS you will be entitled to a rebate of your National Insurance contributions. The rebate is a flat amount **which does not vary by age and sex**. For the 5 years commencing 6 April 1988 the rebate in National Insurance contributions will be 5.8% of band earnings which 2% applies to the employee and 3.8% to the employer.

If you wish to contract-out of SERPS through a personal pension plan you and your employer will continue to pay National Insurance contributions at the contracted-in rate above. However, the Government will pay a sum equal to the flat rate rebate of 5.8% of your band earnings into your personal pension plan, even though the actual cost of providing the equivalent of SERPS (as shown in the above table) might be a lot less than 5.8% of band earnings.

Comparing the flat-rate rebate of 5.8% with the percentages shown in the table above will give you an indication as to whether or not you should contract out. In fact this will only be a rough and ready guide because the payments made by the Government will be enhanced by two further amounts:

1 The employee's share of the rebate, 2%, will be grossed-up to allow for basic rate tax. With basic rate tax at 25% this means that 2% is grossed up to 2.67% of band earnings.
2 If you are contracting-out for the first time the Government will pay an additional 2% incentive.

Thus the total amount which could be paid into a personal pension plan amounts to 8.47% of band earnings as follows:

Employee's share of rebate	2.00%
Tax relief on employee's share	0.67%
Employer's share of rebate	3.80%
2% incentive	2.00%
	8.47%

Once again, if you compare this figure with the table above, contracting-out will become the correct thing to do for a greater number of people.

Contracting-out – an extra year

Although you will not be able to take out a personal pension plan until 1 July 1988 you can still use it to contract-out from 6 April 1987. This means that you are back-dating your decision to contract-out for an extra tax year. The rebate in National Insurance contributions for 1987/88 was 6.25% of band earnings. As described above, the employee's share of the rebate is also grossed-up to allow for basic rate rax (27% in 1987/88) and the Government will also pay an additional 2% incentive if you contract-out for 1987/88.

This means that your personal pension plan can receive an extra 9.05% of band earnings as follows:

Employee's share of rebate	2.15%
Tax relief on employee's share	0.80%
Employer's share of rebate	4.10%
2% incentive	2.00%
	9.05%

The 2% incentive

A personal pension plan which is used to contract-out with effect from 6 April 1987 will be entitled to receive the incentive of 2% of band earnings in respect of the each of the tax years from 6 April 1987 up to 5 April 1993. If you contract-out after 5 April 1988 the 2% incentive will be payable in respect of the tax years in which you are actually contracted-out up to 5 April 1993.

Remember, the 2% incentive is payable to you as an incentive to contract-out of SERPS. If you are *already* contracted-out, there is nothing to stop you taking out a personal pension plan but you *may* not get the 2% incentive:

• If you have been in your company scheme for at least 2 years (and if you can continue to be a member) then you certainly will *not* get the incentive.
• If, however, you change jobs and so leave the scheme, you will get the 2% incentive when you start your new job (provided you take out a personal pension plan and use it to contract-out of SERPS).

Overall, it is a complex area of the legislation and it would be a good idea to take financial advice on this point.

Not a once and for all decision

The decision to contract-out of SERPS is one which you should make on a regular basis. The amount which will be paid by the Government into your personal pension plan will reduce as the years go by. The following data show the contributions which are **likely** to be paid in future years.

1993–1998	–	4.8% of band earnings
1998–2003	–	4.3% of band earnings
2003–2008	–	3.9% of band earnings
2008–2013	–	3.6% of band earnings
2013–2018	–	3.5% of band earnings
2018 onwards	–	3.4% of band earnings

You should note that these figures exclude any tax relief on the employee's share of the rebate. Also, although these percentages reduce as the years go by your band earnings should increase so that the actual cash payments into your personal pension plan will not necessarily reduce.

Of course, these amounts may vary and so it might be in your interest to contract-out for a period and then go back into

SERPS at a later stage. If you compare the current rebate of 8.47% with the figures in Table 2 above you will see that older people would be advised to remain in SERPS. Although it might be advisable for you to contract-out if you are young it is likely that in the future you would be advised to elect to go back into SERPS in order to obtain the best of both worlds.

The important point to remember, however, is that your decision has to be reviewed regularly in the light of hard facts such as the rebate being paid into your personal pension plan, the guarantees being provided by the State and the lack of guarantees under your personal pension plan and perhaps more emotional factors such as whether you value having your own 'pot of gold'.

The following table shows the pensions produced through a personal pension plan (as a percentage of final earnings) by:

- contracting-out until State retirement age.
- remaining in SERPS until State retirement age.
- contracting-out in 1988 and rejoining SERPS after the number of years shown.

EXAMPLE

A woman aged 29 who remains in SERPS could expect to receive a pension of 12.60% of her final earnings. If she were to contract-out until State retirement age her personal pension plan might give her a pension of 15.10% of her final earnings. However, if she were to contract-out through a personal pension plan, and then contract-back in again after 16 years, her total pension might increase to 16.80% of her final earnings.

The table also shows that a woman aged 39 could expect to receive a SERPS pension of 11.70% of her final earnings. If she were to contract-out until State retirement age, however, a personal pension would provide her with only 9.80% of final earnings. Despite this, she should *still* consider contracting-out through a personal pension plan and then contract-back in again after 6 years, as her total pension under these circumstances would amount to 12.90% of her final earnings.

Table 3: Contracting-out or remaining in SERPS – a comparison

Females

Age	Contracting-out to State retirement age %	Remaining in SERPS %	Returning to SERPS after a number of years	%
24	18.30	13.00	21	19.50
29	15.10	12.60	16	16.80
34	12.30	12.10	10	14.60
39	9.80	11.70	6	12.90
44	7.50	11.90	–	–
49	5.30	11.10	–	–

Males

24	24.60	13.60	31	25.10
29	20.60	13.00	24	21.30
34	17.10	12.60	17	18.20
39	13.90	12.10	11	15.50
44	11.10	11.70	6	13.50
49	8.50	11.90	4	12.10
54	6.00	11.10	–	–

Notes

1 It has been assumed that contracting out starts from 1 July 1988 backdated to include the 1987 tax year.
2 The 2% incentive has been included in the above figures.
3 Pensions are shown as a percentage of final earnings assuming that earnings grow at 10% per annum and a future rate of return of 13% per annum.
4 Initial earnings of £10,000 have been assumed.

The break-even point

The ages at which you should decide to remain in SERPS or contract-out depend on a number of factors:

- Will you be entitled to the 2% incentive? (which in any event will not be available beyond 5 April 1993).
- What pension can you expect to receive from your personal pension plan?
- What investment return can you expect to receive on your personal pension plan?

Paying your own contributions

The benefits provided by the DHSS contributions are known as 'protected rights', and certain conditions will apply to them. However, SERPS was never designed to be a complete retirement package and the benefits will almost certainly not be enough. Although contracting-out through a personal pension plan is financially attractive at lower ages (and even at higher ages if you return to SERPS after a period) you should consider taking advantage of all the tax concessions available to you and paying the maximum level of additional contributions to:

- provide more income in retirement,
- ensure that part of your benefits may be taken in a form of a tax-free lump sum. The benefits provided by your protected rights can only be taken as income,
- ensure that if you are ill or disabled contributions can continue to be made to your plan and
- provide life assurance benefits for your dependants if you die before retirement.

Contributions from your employer

If you have taken out a personal pension plan then you must be in non-pensionable employment, ie, your employer is not running an occupational scheme or if he is running one you

are not a member of it. Your employer may have good
reasons for not setting up an occupational pension scheme but
it is possible that he might be willing to pay contributions
directly to your personal pension plan. This will be a matter
for negotiation between you and your employer.

For example, you may prefer a pension contribution to a
bonus payment or payrise. Your employer obtains tax relief on
the pension contribution as it is classed as a business expense
which can be set against his profits, in the same way as a
bonus payment or payrise. (Unfortunately your employer is
unable to pay a contribution directly into one of the existing
retirement annuity contracts but he can give you a payrise
which means that you will have the resources to pay more
into it yourself.)

Total contributions

You will see that contributions can be paid by you, your
employer and the DHSS.

The options above show DHSS contributions buying
'protected rights' which are kept separate from the fund
which is generated by your own contributions and any
employer contributions. Because protected rights are
accumulated through DHSS contributions certain conditions
must apply to the way in which benefits are paid out.

In Chapter 6 we look at the types of benefit which you can
provide through your contribution and employer
contributions and also at protected rights.

Diagram 3: How the protected rights contributions (and any other contributions paid by you or your employer) reach your personal pension plan

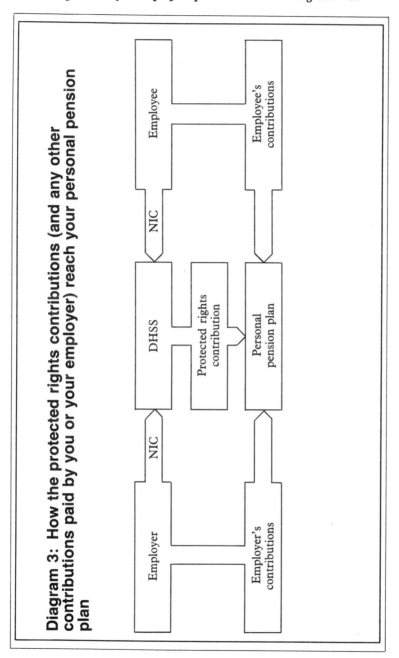

Who should contract-out?

In general terms, it could be to your advantage to contract-out of SERPS if you are less than about age 50 if you are a man, or age 43 if you are a woman.

Diagram 4 assumes that you will be entitled to the special 2% incentive, if you are not (see page 37) the age is reduced to around 47 for a man and 40 for a woman.

How to contract-out

A personal pension plan used purely for contracting-out of SERPS is self-financing. You do not have to dig into your pocket, and nor does your employer. To contract-out all you need to do is to complete a form known as a Joint Notice on which you signify your wish to contract-out of SERPS, specifying the date – always the beginning of a tax year. This form is also completed by the pension provider (which is why it is called a Joint Notice) who will send the form to the Department of Health and Social Security in Newcastle.

After the tax year has ended the DHSS will have received from the Inland Revenue a statement showing the National Insurance contributions which you and your employer have made during the previous tax year. DHSS will then be in a position to calculate the rebate, add to it the tax relief on your share of the rebate, top it up with the 2% incentive if appropriate, and pay the sum directly into your personal pension plan.

The point to make here is that you have to pay the full National Insurance contributions for the whole of the tax year. The rebate is made to your plan at the **end** of the year.

Diagram 4: Who should contract-out?

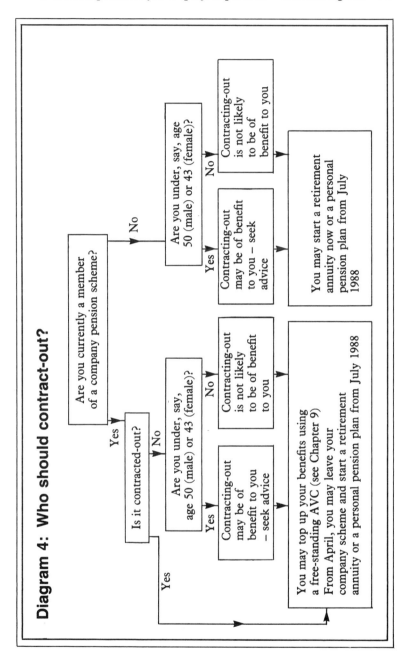

Joint Notice

A Joint Notice is on pp. 39–40.

Maximum contributions to personal pension plans

The maximum contributions which can be paid to a personal pension plan as a percentage of your earnings depend on age, as shown below:

Age on 6 April	Maximum contribution
Up to 50	17.5%
51 to 55	20.0%
56 to 60	22.5%
61 or more	27.5%

The contributions shown above include any made by your employer. However if you wish to contract-out of SERPS the DHSS payments are **in addition** to those set out above.

Tax relief

If you are an employee the contributions which you pay to a personal pension plan are paid net of basic rate tax. For example, if the contributions which you are considering paying amount to £75 per month your contributions will normally be paid by direct debit to the pension provider. The pension provider will then allocate to your pension plan £100

JOINT NOTICE

for beginning payment
of minimum contributions

PERSONAL PENSIONS APP 1

SCHEME MEMBER

What to do

1 Check the information on the back of this form.

2 Read the declaration on this page.

3 If the information is correct, and you agree with the declaration, sign and date the form.

Declaration

I declare that I am, or that I intend to become, a member of the Personal Pension scheme with the number shown in ▮ of this form.

I wish minimum contributions to be paid to this scheme for me from the start date shown in ▮

I understand that the benefits I can get from the State Earnings Related Pension Scheme (SERPS) will be reduced because of these payments of minimum contributions.

Signature

Date

PERSONAL PENSION SCHEME
trustees or managers

Declaration

We declare that the person named on the back of this form is, or intends to become, a member of the Personal Pension scheme with the number shown in ▮ of this form;

that we have agreed to accept this person as a member of the scheme;

that we are willing to receive minimum contributions for this person;

that the date from which we wish minimum contributions to be paid to the scheme for this person is the start date shown in ▮

We claim a £1 payment for any tax week when a payment under section 3 (1) (b) of the Social Security Act 1986 or article 5(1)(b) of the Social Security (Northern Ireland) Order 1986 would otherwise be less than £1.

Name of scheme

Signature by or on behalf of trustees or managers

SPECIMEN

Date

Position

Address for correspondence

PP

1-2

JOINT NOTICE

for beginning payment
of minimum contributions

PERSONAL PENSION SCHEME

1 Scheme number
3-10

2 Start date

Day	Month	Year
06	04	
11-16

SCHEME MEMBER

3 National Insurance number

Letters   Numbers   Letter
17-25

4 Surname
If this has changed in the last
12 months, please give the
previous surname here
26-28

5 Other names
29-30

6 Female ⬜ Male ⬜

7 Date of birth
Please write this in
numbers, not in words
For example 10/10/48

Day   Month   Year
31-36

8 Membership number
in this scheme
37-54

9 Address
Please give the postcode
on the last line of the box

SPECIMEN

Postcode
▧

APP 1

Please make sure both sides   Send the completed   Social Security
of this form have been filled in   form to   COEG
                                                           Newcastle upon Tyne
                                                           NE98 1YX

Printed in the UK for HMSO 12/87 Dd 8043368 3000M 25038

per month recovering the extra £25 directly from the Inland Revenue.

This system, under which relief is given at source, is similar to the method used by banks and building societies when they recover basic rate tax in respect of mortgage interest payments that you make (the MIRAS system). This system means that you obtain tax relief immediately. If you are a higher-rate taxpayer you will have to send a form produced by the pension provider to the Inspector of Taxes who will give you tax relief at the difference between basic rate tax and higher rate tax.

Examples of maximising tax relief are given in Chapter 15.

5 Personal pensions for the self-employed

There are over 2½ million self-employed people in Britain today. If you are one of them, you probably enjoy the freedom of being your own boss, of deciding how you want to spend your working life. There is of course a price to pay for that freedom – you have to take on the responsibilities of an employer – tax payments, insurance, VAT and so on.

Also, you probably spend most of your time taking care of today's problems without thinking about tomorrow's.

It's difficult to be precise about the number of self-employed who aren't preparing for their long-term financial future, but the general view is that there are many. It is estimated that less than a quarter of all self-employed people are making any adequate provision for their future.

So what will you live on? As you have seen, the State will give you something, but it will be the bare minimum. There will be no income from your employer – because **you** are your employer.

If you are self-employed the need for personal pension provision should be of paramount of importance because you will not build up any SERPS pension, unless at some stage during your working life you were an employed person and paid contracted-in contributions at the full rate. The only State benefits payable to you as a self-employed person will be the basic old age pension.

Retirement annuities

Fortunately, you are able to contribute to a retirement annuity contract which you can take out with an insurance company. The contract enjoys all the beneficial tax advantages already mentioned namely:

● you obtain tax relief on the contributions which you pay at your marginal rate of tax,
● the pension fund in which your contributions are invested grows free of UK income and capital taxes,
● when you come to take benefits, between the ages of 60 and 75, part of the fund (approximately one-third) can be paid in the form of a tax-free lump sum with the balance being used to provide you with an income.

Maximum contributions to retirement annuity contracts

The maximum contributions which you may pay to a retirement annuity contract as a percentage of your 'net relevant earnings' depend on age, as shown in the following table:

Age on 6 April	Maximum contribution
Up to 50	17.5%
51 to 55	20.0%
56 to 60	22.5%
61 or more	27.5%

'Earnings' (which are referred to technically as your 'net relevant earnings') means, broadly speaking, your profits minus deductible business expenses.

Tax years and business years

It is important when deciding the level of contributions you wish to pay that you use your net relevant earnings for the appropriate tax year, ie, the period which runs from 6 April to the following 5 April. For example, on 1 June 1988 you may wish to pay a contribution of £2,000 (representing 17.5% of your net relevant earnings of £11,428). This figure would be the amount on which you are paying tax in the tax year 1988/89 but does not necessarily represent your level of profits in that period. This is because the profits on which you are taxed in 1988/89 will normally be your profits in the business year which ended in the previous tax year, ie, 1987/88.

Say that your business year runs from 1 February to 31 January: the figure of £11,428 would be the net profits which you made between 1 February 1987 to 31 January 1988. (Different rules can apply when you start or finish in business.)

Or, if your business year runs from 1 May to 30 April, the figure of £11,428 would be the net profits which you made 1 May 1986 to 30 April 1987. Your net relevant earnings are what the Inland Revenue regards as your profits and it is this figure which can be ascertained from your tax assessment, on which you should base your contributions. You should disregard the profits which your business may be generating now.

Tax relief

The contributions which you pay to the insurance company are the gross contributions and tax relief is obtained through your Tax Inspector. You will obtain a form from the insurance company called a Self-Employed Policy Certificate, (or SEPC form for short) which you should send to the Tax Inspector telling him that you either wish to set the contribution against your net relevant earnings in the *current* tax year or in the *previous* tax year. The Tax Inspector will then either give you a refund of tax or will set the tax relief against tax which you are due to pay.

Chapter 15 gives examples on how to maximise contributions by 'carrying back' to the previous year and also taking advantage of the facility to make up contributions which you could have paid in previous years.

30 June 1988 deadline

From 1 July 1988, the self-employed will be able to provide for their retirement by taking out personal pension plans. Retirement annuity contracts will not be available after 30 June 1988 though, of course, you will be able to continue contributions to a retirement annuity contract that you took out before 1 July 1988.

You may take out a personal pension plan in addition to an existing retirement annuity (provided, of course, that your total contributions do not exceed the maximum). You will also be able to transfer the value of your retirement annuity into your personal pension (but you will not be able to reverse this, ie, you will not be able to transfer the value of your personal pension plan into your retirement annuity).

Although the personal pension plan will look very similar to a retirement annuity contract the latter will allow you to take a higher proportion of tax-free cash at retirement. Because of this you should aim to take out a flexible retirement annuity by 30 June 1988. Flexible retirement annuity contracts allow you to increase contributions at a later stage and these increases will be paid into the original retirement annuity contract. However, if the retirement annuity contract which you took out can accept only level contributions any additional contributions that you wish to pay after 30 June 1988 will have to be directed into a personal pension plan.

A full description of the types of benefits that may be provided under personal pension plans and retirement annuities, and a comparison, is also contained in Chapter 6.

6 The benefits of personal pension plans

'Pensions are too rigid – they require too much planning'.

Personal pension plans are not at all rigid. They now have considerable flexibility and provide for the benefits to emerge out over a period of time rather than all at once (which is what most employed people have to do). You don't actually have to 'retire' to take the benefits, so you can take benefits in stages and gradually wind down to retirement.

Pension

The main purpose of a personal pension plan is to provide you with an income in retirement. 'Retirement' is something of a misnomer as you do not actually have to retire to receive the benefits: you can take benefits at any stage between the ages of 50 and 75 regardless of whether or not you are working.

You can have a number of personal pension plans, enabling you to phase benefits over that period. Alternatively it is likely that some pension providers will be able to supply plans where you can have this flexibility within overall package.

You have the option of using the accumulated fund to purchase an annuity which will be paid during your lifetime or, you may choose a lower pension that continues for the life of your surviving spouse.

For example, £100,000 would purchase the following types of annuity for a man at age 65:

- An annuity of £12,600 a year payable in monthly instalments, but for a minimum of 5 years.
- An annuity of £10,500 a year payable in monthly instalments for a minimum of 5 years increasing each year by 3% compound.
- A joint annuity of £10,300 a year payable in monthly instalments for a minimum of 5 years then during the lives of a man and his wife, who is 3 years younger.

The above annuities assume an underlying interest rate of 10%.

Open market option

You have the right under a personal pension plan to take the accumulated fund and transfer it to an insurance company which is offering the best annuity rates at that time. If you have taken out a personal pension plan with a bank, building society or unit trust the funds **must** be transferred to an insurance company to purchase an annuity.

You agree the amount and payment frequency of the annuity and the date instalments start. Once the annuity comes into payment it is guaranteed. The terms are guaranteed until you (and your spouse for a joint life annuity) die.

Death benefits

Under a personal pension plan death benefits may be provided in the following ways:

- You may contribute up to 5% of your earnings to provide
  for a life assurance benefit to be paid to your dependants
  if you die before your selected retirement date (not later
  than age 75).

This is a very worthwhile benefit as you get tax relief on the
contributions that you pay, unlike normal life assurance
contracts on which no tax relief is given. For example, a man
aged 29 (a non-smoker) who wishes to insure his life for
£100,000 to be payable if he dies before age 60 would have
to pay around £14 per month gross. If he pays basic rate tax
at 25% the net cost is only £10.50. In fact under a personal
pension plan you pay contributions net of basic rate tax so
you only have to find £10.50 per month.

The life assurance benefit may be written 'in trust'. What this
means is that the proceeds belong to your trustees (who must
use the money for your beneficiaries) not to your estate.
Therefore, if you die, the benefits can be paid immediately
to the trustees without them having to wait for probate or
confirmation to be obtained (a process which might take
many months during which time your beneficiaries might
experience financial problems). It is possible to use this life
assurance benefit as collateral for a mortgage as explained in
Chapter 11.

- The contributions which you have been paying into your
  personal pension plan may be returned if you die before
  your selected retirement age. In some plans you may
  receive only the contributions which you have paid. With
  others, the plan may provide for the total value of the
  fund, including investment growth, to be returned. As
  with the life assurance benefit mentioned in the previous
  paragraph, this benefit may also be written in trust.

Putting the life cover benefits in trust is a very sensible
precaution. This not only ensures that your beneficiaries get
immediate access to the funds (which could be needed), but
also that the proceeds are *not* included in your estate for
inheritance tax purposes. This can be important – inheritance

tax starts to bite on relatively low levels and a large tax bill can easily arise at a most unwelcome time.

Waiver of contribution benefit

If you are unable to work because you are sick or disabled it is likely that your earnings may dry up. If you are employed it is possible that your employer might pay you for a limited period, eg, 3 months or 6 months. If you are self-employed the situation might become even more acute.

In either case a lengthy absence from work could seriously jeopardise your future financial independence. Obviously, if you have no earnings then you would be unable to contribute to your personal pension plan.

Waiver of contribution benefit ensures that your contributions to your personal pension plan are maintained on your behalf by the insurance company for as long as you cannot work due to disability. However, this particular benefit does not provide you with an **income** when you are sick or disabled but merely maintains the contributions that you would have paid yourself (although, in one sense waiver of contribution **does** provide you with an income: it ensures that your **retirement** income is intact).

For example, the pension that would be payable for a man aged 65 if he commenced paying annual contributions of £1,000 at age 40, but missed two contributions at ages 42 and 43 because he was disabled would amount to approximately £14,700 per annum.

If he had included waiver of contribution benefit within the annual contribution of £1,000, the pension at retirement would amount to approximately £17,700 per annum.

The waiver of contribution benefit for a man of this age would cost around 3% of the contribution for pension benefits (although the exact figure will vary from insurer to insurer), and the extra contribution is eligible for tax relief.

Disability benefits

Although pensions under personal pension plans may not commence until age 50, in the event of *permanent incapacity* pensions may start immediately. However, the pension itself is unlikely to be adequate, being based on only the fund built up by the contributions paid to date.

Alternatively, it is possible to insure against disability through permanent incapacity. As with waiver of contribution benefit, the cost of providing disability benefit is eligible for tax relief.

Tax-free cash

One of your most valuable options under a personal pension plan will be the facility to take up to one quarter of the accumulated fund in the form of a tax-free lump sum. The remaining three-quarters of the fund is used to purchase your pension. Even if the remaining pension is likely to be insufficient you should still consider taking the tax-free cash and invest it elsewhere to top-up your pension (see Chapter 12).

The facility to take tax-free cash may enable you to arrange a pension related mortgage, an extremely attractive option (see Chapter 11).

Protected rights

Although it is possible to contract-out of SERPS through a personal pension plan, the Government retains an interest in how the benefits generated by its contributions are paid out. Protected rights are subject to the following conditions:

- no part of the fund may be taken in the form of a tax-free lump sum;
- the pension must commence at State pension age (60 for a woman, 65 for a man) and no earlier and must increase in payment at the lower of 3% per annum and inflation as measured by the Retail Prices Index; the pension may be deferred up to age 75;
- the pension must not discriminate between males and females, and between single and married people;
- if the person who was receiving the pension dies, it must continue to the spouse. At this stage the level of the spouse's pension must be one half of the original pension.

You will see from the points above that no provision is made for early retirement, tax-free cash on retirement and lump sum life assurance benefits to be paid to dependants.

The only way this can be achieved is to make sure that your personal pension plan does not provide just 'protected rights'. You need to ensure that either you pay additional contributions yourself or that you get your employer to pay contributions (or a combination of the two).

Funding for cash through protected rights

An extremely tax-efficient option is to contract-out from SERPS and pay additional contributions which will generate an additional fund which may be taken completely tax free.

EXAMPLE

A woman contracts-out through a personal pension plan and at age 60 her protected rights amount to a fund of £125,000 of which £100,000 is used to provide her with a pension and £25,000 is used to provide for a widower's pension. No part of this fund may be taken in cash.

She pays additional contributions to the plan which generate an additional fund of £33,333 (this is not regarded as protected rights).

The total fund at age 60 amounts to £158,333.

Under a personal pension plan up to 25% of the fund used to provide the member's benefit may be taken tax free: £25,000 of the protected rights fund is required to provide a widower's pension leaving £133,333 used to provide the member's benefits. 25% of this may be taken tax free, ie, £33,333. The protected rights fund is not being eroded.

Thus, the contributions paid by her into the personal pension plan have received tax relief, the total funds have accumulated tax free and at age 60 the fund built up by her contributions may be taken completely tax free making this an unsurpassable investment.

Pension planning in stages

A combination of all the ideas that have been discussed in this chapter provide the framework for a planned approach to providing your pension if your finances are a little stretched in the early years:

1 You should consider taking out a personal pension plan funded by the DHSS rebate. This will provide you with a protected rights annuity with no additional outlay required on your behalf.
2 You should then consider making additional contributions to 'fund for cash' as described in the previous section.
3 Further stages could involve you paying additional

contributions to provide for life assurance benefits to be paid to your dependants if you die before retirement; waiver of contribution benefit and sufficient funds enable you to take additional tax-free cash and a pension from age 50 onwards.

This is the sort of approach which the new legislation offers you – and, of course, the additional contributions could be paid by you, and or by your employer.

Comparison of retirement annuities and personal pension plans

The following is a brief comparison of the major differences between a retirement annuity and a personal pension plan:

Table 4		
	Retirement annuity	*Personal pension plan*
Benefit ages	*Between 60 and 75*	*Between 50 and 75*
Basis of calculating tax-free cash	3 × the annuity remaining after cash has been taken*	25% of fund†
Facility to carry back/ carry forward contributions?	Yes	Yes
Ancillary benefits, eg, life assurance, waiver of contribution?	Yes	Yes
Ability to contract-out?	No	Yes
Cash limit?	£150,000 (unless effected before 17 March 1987)	£150,000
Tax relief on contributions at source?	No	Yes, for employed persons

	Retirement annuity	Personal pension plan
Ability to accept employer contributions?	No	Yes
Facility to accept transfers from other schemes?	No	Yes
Facility to pay transfers to other schemes?	Yes	Yes
Ability to put life assurance benefit in trust?	Yes	Yes
Open market option available?	Yes	Yes

* This rather complicated method of calculating the tax-free cash under a retirement annuity (3 × the annuity remaining after the cash has been taken) will be replaced by a simple method for the personal pension plan – 25% of the fund. Although simpler, the tax-free cash will generally be lower than under a retirement annuity.

† Any part of the fund which is used to buy a widow's or widower's annuity may have to be excluded from the total fund for this purpose which means that, in practice, around only 20% may be taken tax free.

Assuming a retirement fund of £100,000 the amounts which could be taken in the form of tax-free cash are as follows:

Table 5

		Retirement annuity	Personal pension plan
Man aged	60	£27,600	£25,000
	65	£29,500	£25,000
	70	£32,100	£25,000
Woman aged	60	£25,600	£25,000
	65	£27,000	£25,000
	70	£29,100	£25,000

Notes

1 You will see that under the retirement annuity the tax-free sum increases as age increases, and differs according to sex.

2 In arriving at the tax-free cash under the retirement annuity an underlying interest rate of 10% has been assumed. If interest rates were lower than, say, 8% the tax-free cash under the retirement annuity could be lower than £25,000 at the younger ages.

3 If you exercise the open market option under a retirement annuity and transfer to a personal pension plan your tax-free cash will be limited to 25% of the fund.

4 The column showing tax-free cash sums of £25,000 assures that a widow's and widower's annuity is not required. Otherwise, the figure would reduce by around 15% to £21,000, depending on the ages of the husband and wife.

7 Retirement planning – comparing forms of investment

'Pensions are money down the drain'.

Money put into a pension isn't available to spend now, it's true. But money paid into a pension is doubly tax-free: tax-free when you pay it in and tax-free while it grows in value. You pay no tax on the money that goes from your income into your pension, and the money invested on your behalf by a pension fund pays no income tax, no capital gains tax and no corporation tax. Pensions are money in the bank. Tax-free.

Traditional methods of saving

It is quite likely that over the years you have saved in a number of ways. You probably have a couple of building society accounts, and you may have National Savings Certificates or a National Savings Investment Account.

You may also have invested in endowment insurance policies which combine an element of life assurance but with the main purpose of building up a nest-egg at the end of, say, 15 years.

In recent years you may have become more speculative by investing directly into the Stock Market. Perhaps the special deals given to investors in nationalised industries when they were sold off by the Government appealed to you.

You may even have channelled your savings into a time-share apartment in the sun, or a holiday home in the UK to which you will retire some day.

The prospect of attractive returns by investing in the Stock Market but at the same time reducing the level of risk through a spread of investments might have encouraged you to consider unit trusts.

The above investments carry varying degrees of risk, from the building society at one end of the spectrum to the stocks and shares at the other end. What all these investments have in common, however, is the fact that they have been paid for out of your after-tax income. For example, assuming that the top slice of your income is taxed at 25% only £750 would be left for you to invest out of £1,000 of earned income. Similarly, if you are paying tax at 40% only £600 would be left for you to invest.

In addition, if you are a higher rate taxpayer, you will be liable to pay further tax on the income from your investments, for example from your building society account, unit trusts, stocks and shares (but not qualifying endowment assurance policies where higher rate tax is not normally payable on the proceeds at the end of the term). When you sell your stocks and shares or unit trusts, you may have a capital gains tax bill if you sell at a profit.

Saving through pensions

Contributions which you pay to an occupational pension scheme, including 'Additional Voluntary Contributions' (see Chapter 9) and contributions which you pay to personal pension plans have a great advantage because they are paid out of your gross income. This means that £1,000 could be invested into your personal pension plan as compared with £750 into a non-pension investment if you are a 25% taxpayer.

In other words 33% more is invested. The tax advantages
do not end there.

The pension fund grows free of tax because the people
investing the pension fund money – the pension plan trustees
– do not have to pay income tax on these investments. Also,
they do not have to pay capital gains tax when they sell the
pension fund investments. The combination of tax relief on
contributions and tax-free income and capital gains results
in significant advantages over other forms of saving (see the
following examples).

However, there is one snag with the pension investment.
There are certain restrictions on when you can take the benefits
and it may not be possible to take the whole of it in the form
of a tax-free lump sum. Under a personal pension plan only
one quarter may be taken tax-free and the balance must be
used to provide an annuity which, of course, dies with you
unless it continues to your dependants. This is in contrast to
a building society investment for example, where you can
continue to draw interest off your remaining account and in
the event of your death the account forms part of your estate.

Suppose, for example, you decide to invest £100 a month out
of your take-home pay into a building society. To do this, you
have to earn £133 a month, because tax (at 25%) will take the
first £33. Your building society investment will then earn
interest at, say 6½% (which is equivalent to 8½% to a basic
rate taxpayer) and this would mean that a regular monthly
investment of £100 would grow to about £73,000 (after
reinvestment of the net interest after all taxes) over 25 years.

However, you could equally afford to put the entire £133 a
month into a pension plan (because you pay no tax on
pension contributions) and your overall financial position will
be the same – the money left out of your take-home pay is
reduced by only £100 a month. In addition, your pension
fund investments will also earn income but this is tax-free
as well. Consequently, (and assuming the *same* rate of
investment return as the building society) your pension fund

contributions of £133 per month could be worth over £110,000 in 25 years time.

If you are a higher rate taxpayer, the difference is even more pronounced. A 40% taxpayer could afford to invest £167 a month into a pension plan and be no worse off in take-home pay than investing £100 into a building society. In addition, the building society interest would be liable to further tax which means that the overall fund at the end of 25 years would be reduced to just under £60,000 (after reinvestment of the net interest after all taxes) whereas the pension fund on the other hand would be worth about £170,000.

It will be seen from the above example that the tax advantages of pension plans are considerable. This is why limits are imposed by the Inland Revenue on the contributions that you can pay into them. Under personal pension plans there is a limit on contributions of around 17.5% of your earnings (though this is increased for older people). Under occupational schemes there is a limit on the eventual pension of two-thirds of your final pay.

The reality of those 'telephone numbers'

Your initial impression on looking at the above figures may be that you could never see a need for a lump sum of say £170,000 per annum in 25 years' time. As a result of this you would call into question whether you really had to spend £100 per month net in pension planning. However, it is important however to look at the purchasing power of those amounts in today's terms. The following table shows what £1,000 would be worth in today's terms over a range of years and at a range of different inflation rates.

For example, if inflation is at 6% per annum over the next 25 years, that sum of £170,000 is worth £39,609 in today's terms (£170,000 multiplied by 233 and divided by 1,000).

Table 6

Period (years)	3% Inflation	6% Inflation	9% Inflation
1	971	943	917
2	913	890	842
3	915	840	772
4	888	792	708
5	863	747	650
10	744	558	422
15	642	417	275
20	554	312	178
25	478	233	116
30	412	174	75
35	355	130	49
40	307	97	32

Similarly, the sum of £73,000 in 25 years time is worth £17,009 in today's terms, and £110,000 is worth £25,630 in today's terms.

8 Occupational pension schemes

'Pensions are a luxury'.

A significant number of people who retire and take their old age pension haven't got enough to live on. In survey after survey, one of the most consistent comments made by retired people is that they wished they'd started planning earlier. Many people cannot live on the state old age pension in anything approaching comfort and they rely on other sources of income.

Our retirement can only be as good as the plans we make for it. If you think pensions are a luxury, consider what luxuries you might have to give up if your retirement pension is inadequate.

Defined benefit schemes

Around one half of the working population are members of occupational schemes. This includes people who work in the private sector and also those working in the public sector, for example, civil servants, policemen, nurses, firemen, and the armed forces. If you are a member of an occupational scheme it is likely that you are already contracted-out of SERPS – because your employer made the decision that you should be contracted-out by setting up an occupational scheme which provided benefits at least equal to what SERPS would have given you.

Contracting-out through occupational pension schemes commenced in 1978. Many schemes which had been in existence prior to that time required only minor amendments to make them suitable for contracting-out in 1978. If you are contracted-out you and your employer will be paying National Insurance contributions at the contracted-out rate.

The scheme will be a 'final salary' scheme, sometimes known as a '**defined benefit**' scheme. This means that your pension is defined as a percentage of your income at or around retirement, eg, 1/60th or 1/80th of your final salary for each year of service to retirement. Part of this pension will be called a 'guaranteed minimum pension' (or GMP) which matches the pension to which you would have been entitled if you had not been contracted-out. This type of scheme involves your employer in an open-ended liability because your ultimate benefits will be based on your future earnings which are unknown, making it difficult to quantify costs.

However, it is likely that you will be required to contribute towards the cost of the scheme, for example 5% of your pay, with your employer meeting the balance of the cost of the benefits. If you are not sure if you are contracted-out check your National Insurance contributions which are itemised on your payslip or read the booklet which you should have received from your employer describing the benefits under your occupational scheme.

Defined contribution schemes

You may be a member of a defined contribution scheme, often known as 'money purchase' scheme. The benefits will not be related to your salary at retirement but will depend upon the contributions paid into the scheme by your employer on your behalf, any contributions which you make in addition, and the investment growth on those contributions. For example, your employer may be paying a percentage of your pay or a contribution which may vary from year to year depending on his profits. Until 6 April 1988 these types of schemes could not be used to contract-out of SERPS.

However, in order to increase the numbers of people contracted-out and to encourage employers to set up occupational schemes for employees without involving employers in an open-ended liability (which is inherent in the defined benefit approach), the Government now permits defined contribution schemes or money purchase schemes to be used to contract-out. These schemes are known as COMPS, ie, 'contracted-out money purchase schemes'.

They operate on similar principles to personal pension plans taken out by individuals in the sense that an element of the eventual benefits is classed as 'protected rights'. As with personal pension plans protected rights are generated by contributions representing the rebate in National Insurance Contributions applicable to people who are contracted-out. However, there is a small difference.

With personal pension plans the DHSS calculates the rebate and pays it directly into your personal pension plan after the tax year in question has ended. Under COMPS, both you and your employer pay reduced National Insurance Contributions, at the contracted-out rate. Your employer is required to pay the difference between contracted-in and contracted-out rates directly into the scheme on your behalf. These contributions will then generate protected rights for each individual member. It is likely that your employer will pay additional contributions to provide additional benefits, eg, death in service benefits, or an additional pension to top up the protected rights.

A contracted-out money purchase scheme may also include members who are not contracted-out. As with personal pension plans, contracting-out under a money purchase basis favours younger people (see Table 3 in Chapter 4). When it becomes advisable for you to go back into SERPS you do not have to leave the money purchase scheme but merely cease to be contracted-out.

Leaving your company pension scheme

Many occupational schemes provide excellent benefits and pension scheme trustees keep members and pensioners fully informed at regular intervals of scheme developments such as changes in Inland Revenue practice, how much the scheme is worth, how much the employer is contributing and the value of your prospective benefits and so on.

From 6 April 1988 however, it will be possible for you to leave your employer's scheme if you wish and it will not be possible for employers to make entry into the pension scheme a condition of employment. Generally though, if you are a member of your employer's scheme **you are going to be better off remaining a member**.

If you leave the scheme, or decide not to join in the first place, you will have the following options:

- to make no private provision at all, but to rely purely on the State: (this would almost certainly amount to a complete abdication of responsibility),
- to take out a personal pension plan (or a retirement annuity if this decision faces you before 1 July 1988).

If you take out a personal pension plan you may wish to use it for contracting-out of SERPS and receive contributions directly from the DHSS on the basis set out in Chapter 4. If you are at an age when contracting-out of SERPS would not be to your advantage you can still take out a personal pension plan and contribute to it yourself.

It is possible that your employer might be prepared to contribute to your personal pension plan as he will not be contributing on your behalf to the occupational pension scheme as you have opted out of it. On the other hand, your employer might wish to deter you from opting out of his scheme by refusing to contribute to your personal pension plan or by refusing to allow you to come back into the pension scheme at a later stage.

Although employers may refuse to pay contributions into personal pension plans when the option first becomes available or over the next few years, it is likely that after a period employers will become more accustomed to recruiting people who have taken out personal pension plans in the past and who wish to keep them going. In the future many employees will negotiate employers' contributions on taking up employment.

It is possible that during the period approaching 6 April 1988, when many of the changes affecting occupational pension schemes came about, your employer asked you to sign a form stating that you wished to join, or remain a member of the scheme: if you did sign a 'statement of intent' there is nothing in law to prevent you changing your mind later on and opting-out of the scheme.

Should you leave your employer's scheme?

The factors that you should consider in deciding whether or not to remain in your employer's scheme will vary according to your personal circumstances and the benefits provided by the scheme but in general the following points should be considered:

- If you leave your company pension scheme and take out a personal pension plan will your employer contribute to it?
- What benefits will you be giving up if you leave? Scheme benefits can vary enormously: for example the scheme might provide benefits of a pension of 1/80th of final pay for each year of service, a lump sum life assurance benefit if you die in service of twice your salary and a dependant's pension of one half of your pension payable in the event

of your death, and pensions in payment might increase at, say, 3% per annum. Alternatively, the scheme might provide, say, a pension which accrues at 1/50th of final pay for each year of service with a life assurance benefit of 4 times your salary plus dependants' pensions of two-thirds of your pension payable in the event of your death, post retirement increases in line with inflation and good benefits for members who leave the scheme before retirement.

To find out the level of your scheme benefits you should look at your explanatory booklet and the regular statement that your scheme trustees have to provide you with once a year.

- Is the pension scheme contributory?
- Does the scheme provide benefits on a money purchase basis (the basis which applies under personal pension plans)?
- Are you likely to remain in the scheme until retirement or are you likely to have a series of jobs before retirement (in which case a personal pension plan may be more suitable)?
- Are the transfer values offered to early leavers who wish to transfer their accrued benefits to other schemes attractive?
- If you leave will your employer allow you to rejoin at a later date?

Generally speaking, leaving a good company scheme will only be a proposition for younger people who intend to move jobs before settling down to a long-term career. Overall, you should think *very* carefully before leaving your company scheme and take financial advice before you do. It would be hard, for example, to think of any reason why it would be sensible to leave a non-contributory scheme (unless the benefits were particularly poor).

Additional Voluntary Contributions

Rather than leaving your employer's scheme it may be better
for you to remain in the scheme and top-up the benefits by
paying AVCs. 'AVC' is short for Additional Voluntary
Contribution, ie, additional contributions which you are
allowed to pay to your employer's scheme to increase your
benefits, or perhaps to buy benefits not provided in the
scheme.

AVCs are covered in Chapter 9.

If your employer's scheme is not contracted-out you can take
out a free-standing AVC and use it to contract-out personally
on a basis which is very similar to contracting-out through
personal pension plans (see Chapter 4). This means that if
you are young you obtain all the benefits of contracting-out
personally whilst remaining a member of your employer's
occupational scheme.

Death in service benefits

If you leave your employer's occupational scheme it is possible
that you will lose out on death in service benefits provided
under the scheme. This usually comprises a lump sum payable
on the event of your death before retirement of up to 4 times
your pay, and a widow's or widower's pension.

However, some employers may continue to provide you with
death in service benefits even if you leave the scheme. It is
permissible for your employer to provide you with death in
service benefits in this way and for you to take out a personal
pension plan to provide your pension benefits.

Public sector employees

If you are employed in the public sector you will also have
the choice of leaving your scheme. It is unlikely that it will
be in your interests to do so as many of these schemes provide
inflation-proofing of benefits when they come into payment.
Also, there has been no indication that public sector
employers would be willing to contribute to individual
personal pension plans taken out by employees.

Public sector schemes operate slightly differently from private
sector schemes. Under a private sector scheme, benefits are
usually expressed as a pension which is payable at retirement,
part of which you exchange, or commute, for a tax-free lump
sum. On the other hand, public sector schemes, usually
provide a pension of, say, 1/80th of final pay for each year
of service, giving a maximum pension of around one half of
final pay *plus* a tax-free lump sum.

You will also be able to top up your benefits through voluntary
contributions either within the scheme or, outside the
scheme, through a free-standing AVC (see Chapter 9).

9 Additional Voluntary Contributions

'It's better to save elsewhere'.

Saving elsewhere may give you more immediate access to the cash if you need it but there are few alternative forms of investment that can compete on tax grounds. For example, if you're paying basic rate of tax, you can save £75 out of every £100 that you earn. If it goes into your pension plan, you save the whole £100 – and the income earned by your savings is tax-free as well.

If you are a member of an occupational scheme, whether in the public or private sector, you will have the right to pay additional contributions to top up your benefits from 6 April 1988.

Even if the scheme is non-contributory, ie, where your employer does not require you to contribute towards the cost of the benefits, you will still have the option of paying additional contributions.

Inland Revenue limits

Inland Revenue limits are two-pronged: the total contributions that you may pay to an occupational scheme amount to 15% of your pay (pay includes your basic salary plus other items which might fluctuate such as bonuses, commissions, and also the taxable element of fringe benefits such as your company car, company-paid petrol, etc). If you are required to contribute 5% of your pay under the occupational scheme this means that you have the facility to pay additional voluntary contributions of 10% of your pay. If the scheme is non-contributory then you may pay additional voluntary contributions of up to 15% of your pay.

However, the total benefits payable under the scheme are subject to Inland Revenue limits as follows (for full details see Chapter 14):

- Your pension at retirement must not exceed two-thirds of your final pay.
- Part of this pension may be exchanged for a tax-free lump sum not exceeding 1½ times your final pay, subject to an overall maximum lump sum of £150,000.
- If you die during retirement a pension of up to two-thirds of your pension may by provided for your widow or widower.
- If you die in service a pension may be provided for your widow or widower and dependants but based on the maximum prospective pension that you could have received if you had lived until retirement.
- If you die in service a lump sum life assurance benefit of 4 times your pay may be provided.

Any additional contributions that you make to the scheme have to be limited to make sure that the above benefit limits are not exceeded. Your scheme trustee or administrator will be able to tell you what additional contributions you may pay and will also warn you if there is a likelihood that Inland Revenue limits might be exceeded.

In-house AVCs

The AVC facility offered by your employer will normally take the form of a separate 'account' within the occupational scheme. The employer will collect your additional contributions (along with any contractual contributions that you are expected to pay) by deducting the gross contributions from your pay and calculating your income tax on the net amount which remains. This is known as a 'net pay arrangement' and means that you get immediate tax relief.

Your contributions will then be invested in the pension fund in the usual way to top-up whatever combination of benefits are allowed by the facility which will normally include one of the following:

- *An insurance policy:* in this case the contributions are collected by your employer but paid directly to an insurance company which will invest the contributions in an insurance policy on your life.
- *An individual 'account':* interest is paid on your account reflecting interest rates credited by building societies (except that you get a higher return because of the tax advantages of pension schemes). In fact, your contributions might be directed to a special account with a specific building society.
- *Added years:* your employer might credit you with 'added years', ie, additional years of service under the scheme. This method is common under public sector schemes. The scheme actuary will have calculated a table showing the additional years of service that may be bought for a given level of contribution.

This might prove to be the best option for you if your pay increases significantly, eg, through promotion or in periods of high inflation. However, 'added years' are normally expensive to buy as the actuary has to take into account in advance the cost to the occupational scheme of inflation-proofing your additional years' benefits.

- A combination of building society related investments and insurance policies.

Some employers offer employees the option of investing in a combination of these types of investments. Although this type of facility is preferable to one which offers only a limited choice you do not have complete freedom of choice as to where your additional voluntary contributions are invested.

Free-standing AVCs

This is a new type of AVC contribution permitted by the Inland Revenue for members of occupational schemes with effect from 26 October 1987. The expression 'free-standing' is a rather odd one as you have to be accruing benefits under another scheme (assume it is called the 'main scheme') before you can have a free-standing AVC scheme. You have complete freedom of choice as to where your additional contributions are invested, rather than being restricted to the types of options that normally apply to in-house arrangements, as described in the previous section.

There are a number of points to be aware of:

- Provided you are accruing benefits under a main scheme you will be entitled to take out a free-standing AVC contract with a pension provider of your own choice, (ie, an insurance company, building society, bank or unit trust).
- The contract will be a personal contract between you and the pension provider. Your employer or the main scheme trustees will not be involved at this stage.
- Your contributions will be paid to the pension provider net of basic rate tax (in the same way as personal contributions to a personal pension plan as described in Chapter 4). If you are a higher rate taxpayer you obtain basic rate tax relief at source but you will have to send a form (given to you by the pension provider) to the Inland Revenue to reclaim higher rate tax.
- The trustee of the main scheme will be required to send a completed questionnaire to your pension provider estimating the maximum additional voluntary contributions that you may pay, without exceeding Inland Revenue limits. The pension provider will also re-check this information if you wish to increase your AVCs and will do this automatically during the 10 years leading up to your normal retirement date, at 3 yearly intervals.

- Your free-standing AVC contract may not be used to provide tax-free cash on retirement. It may only provide a pension at retirement for you and/or your dependants, although it is possible to provide additional death in service life assurance benefits.
- Your total personal contributions are limited to 15% of your pay (this includes any contractual contributions that you pay to the main scheme and any additional voluntary contributions that you might be paying to an in-house AVC scheme).
- Your employer is not allowed to contribute to your free-standing AVC scheme.
- Only one free-standing AVC scheme may be taken out in any tax year.
- If you are a 20% director (see Chapters 13 and 14), ie, a director who controls his company, you are not eligible for a free-standing AVC.

The free-standing AVC contract is an excellent means of boosting your retirement income. You have freedom of choice as to where you invest – you are not tied to the facility offered by your employer under his own in-house scheme and, if you wish, you can change pension providers each tax year.

Contracting-out through a free-standing AVC

You also have the facility of using your free-standing AVC contract to contract-out personally—a very worthwhile benefit if you are a member of an occupational scheme which is not contracted-out. If you use your free-standing AVC to contract-out the following factors must be borne in mind:

- The benefits generated by the DHSS contributions have to be taken into account in arriving at Inland Revenue limits, (described at the beginning of this chapter, and in detail in Chapter 14).

• When the DHSS pay contributions into your AVC scheme there will be **no** tax relief on your share of the rebate contributions, (as applies when DHSS contributions are paid into a personal pension plan).

Currently the total amount that may be paid into your free-standing AVC contract for 1987/88 and for 1988/93 will be as follows:

Table 7		
	1987/88	*1988/93*
Employee's share of rebate	2.15%	2.00%
Employer's share of rebate	4.10%	3.80%
2% incentive where appropriate	2.00%	2.00%
	8.25%	7.80%

10 Changing jobs

The effect on your pension

These days people change jobs much more frequently than they did in the past or leave the service of one employer without joining a new employer. This is partly because of economic conditions which have resulted in the huge increase in unemployment in recent years and also because of the nature of some jobs where people move from employer to employer regularly to extend their experience and earnings potential.

Changing jobs can affect your pension, although your pension is probably the last thing that you are thinking about when you are considering leaving one employer and joining another, especially if you are young and have little interest in pensions anyway. But, as you get older you may regret not having spent more time considering your pension provision as the effect that a job move might have on your pension benefits may actually deter you from moving.

In 1987 the Government brought in changes to the pensions legislation which by increasing the length of service required to qualify for a full pension from your company scheme (from 10 years to 20 years), may actually reduce job mobility for some people.

In the past many pension schemes discriminated against the early leaver. However, the Government introduced improvements to benefit early leavers in the Social Security Act 1985 although problems still remain in this area.

Most occupational schemes will require that you complete at least 2 years pensionable service before becoming entitled to pension benefits. Prior to 6 April 1988 you usually had to complete 5 years' pensionable service. Some schemes give 'vested rights' immediately on joining the scheme: this means that regardless of when you leave you will be entitled to the benefits accrued up to the date of leaving.

Options on leaving

If you leave your job you will usually have a number of options regarding your pension. These are explained in the following pages but the overall position is somewhat complicated. Therefore, it would be good advice to get a clear statement from your *new* employer on the arrangements he is prepared to set up on your behalf and for you to negotiate the best deal you can for your *current* employer. It is an area where competent financial advice is needed.

Paid-up benefits

This means that your existing fund 'freezes' and no further contributions are paid into it.

A reduced pension will be payable from your normal retirement date as specified under the rules of the scheme (normally age 60 for women, 65 for men). If, for example, you were a member of a 'defined benefit' pension scheme which provided you with a pension of 1/60th of your final pay for each year of service (where your final pay is calculated at or around retirement) and you leave service early at age 38 having joined at age 30, you will be entitled to a reduced pension, (or a 'paid-up' pension) of 8/60ths of your final pay. Your final pay, however, will be defined at or around the date of leaving the scheme.

Your pension, however, is not completely 'frozen'. In recent legislation the Government introduced rules which mean that your pension benefits have to be increased at a rate of 5% per year compound or in line with the Retail Price Index, whichever is the lower. This is called 'revaluation'.

However, revaluation only applies to pension benefits that have built up since 1 January 1985. In the above example, it was assumed that you had completed 8 years' service since joining the company. If you left on 1 January 1988, you would have completed 3 years' service under the legislation – therefore, 3/8 of your paid-up pension would fall under the new legislation and would have to be revalued each year.

Also, if the employer used the scheme to contract out of SERPS, the paid-up pension will include a 'guaranteed minimum pension' – ie, the pension which you would have got from SERPS if you had not been contracted-out. This GMP element must also be revalued between the date of leaving and normal retirement date. Normally the revaluation is 8½% per annum compound in respect of your years of service up to 5 April 1988 and 7½% per annum compound in respect of any years of service from 6 April 1988 up to normal retirement date.

If you were a member of a 'money purchase' pension scheme you will be entitled to the benefits secured by the contributions paid up to the date of leaving.

A refund of contributions

If you leave service voluntarily before completing 2 years' pensionable service you are not generally entitled to any benefits unless the scheme is 'contributory', in which case your personal contributions will be returned to you, generally without any investment growth, and subject to a tax deduction of 20%.

It is important to realise that if you take a refund of your contributions this does not make the period of your service with the employer 'non-pensionable'. If, later, you wish to start a retirement annuity or personal pension plan you will not be able to pay additional contributions for the period when you were in the occupational scheme even though you have received a refund of your contributions.

Transfer values

As an alternative to a paid-up pension you have the right to transfer the value of your accrued benefits to another scheme. This right was introduced by the Social Security Act 1985 and applies if you leave service from 1 January 1986. (If you have a number of small paid-up pensions under occupational schemes which you left before 1 January 1986 you can approach the trustees of these schemes to see if they will allow you to transfer the benefits but they are not obliged to do so.)

Transfer values are generally the cause of many complaints about the benefits offered to early leavers. You might expect the transfer value to represent the contributions which you and the employer have paid into the scheme on your behalf during your period of membership, together with the investment growth that has accrued. In practice, most occupational schemes do not grant transfer values on such a favourable basis, although some do. Instead, most transfer values are calculated on the basis of the amount of money which would have to be invested now at a given rate of interest, to accumulate a sum of money which would purchase the paid-up pension calculated as above, at normal retirement date. The rate of interest which is assumed in the calculations can make a considerable difference to the transfer value you are offered.

There is a code of practice adopted by scheme trustees designed to give equity between people wishing to take transfer values from occuptional schemes and other people wishing to transfer money into occupational pension schemes. The reasoning behind this code of practice is that the rate of interest used for transfer values should have regard to market rates of interest. For example, if interest rates are high the value of your paid up pension under the occupational pension scheme would be on the low side. Although the calculated transfer value would be low the theory is that under the same investment conditions the new occuptional pension scheme should be able to apply this transfer value to provide similar benefits.

Section 32 annuities

Under the Social Security Act 1986 you have a right to ask the trustees of your company scheme to 'buy out' their liability to provide scheme benefits by purchasing an annuity for you with an insurance company in accordance with section 32 of the Finance Act 1981 – hence the expression 'section 32 annuities'. These are sometimes known as 'buy-out bonds'. You also have the right to choose the insurance company.

The Section 32 annuity must provide benefits within Inland Revenue limits, and will normally match the paid-up pension which would have been provided under the scheme, although it might provide higher benefits. You will have to compare the terms and conditions of Section 32 annuities offered by insurance companies before asking the trustees to purchase the Section 32 annuity of your choice.

Personal pension plans

If you leave your employer's scheme from 1 July 1988 onwards you will also have the option of transferring your benefits into a personal pension plan (as described in Chapter 4). Although a personal pension plan is generally only available if you are self-employed or in non-pensionable employment there is an exception: even if you are in a pension scheme you can take out a personal pension plan which is funded soley by the transfer from another scheme.

This new option will be more flexible than the section 32 annuity described above because your transferred benefits will be subject to the personal pension legislation. for example, you will be able to take the benefits in stages between ages 50 and 75.

If you were a member of a contracted out defined benefit scheme your transfer will include a guaranteed minimum pension (GMP). On transferring into the personal pension there will no longer be any need for the 'guarantee' to continue but 'protected rights' will have to be provided instead.

Surpluses

In recent years many pension schemes, mainly those of large public companies, have generated surpluses, usually because the scheme funds have grown at a significantly higher rate than the earnings of the scheme members and because of shrinking workforces. In order to reduce these surpluses (a course of action forced on companies by the Inland Revenue) some pension schemes have improved the benefits of members, including those who have left service.

If your pension scheme has a surplus, but the methods of reducing it have not yet been decided, it might be advisable to retain your interest in the scheme in the form of paid-up benefits, rather than taking a transfer value to your new scheme. If you later find that the surplus is to be reduced by, say, a 'contribution holiday', with no improvement in members' benefits you can go ahead with the transfer at that time. If your benefits are improved your transfer value will be higher.

Transferability between schemes

Although there have been no Inland Revenue restrictions on the transfer of monies between approved occupational schemes, it has not been possible to transfer monies between occupational schemes and retirement annuities. Your only option is to transfer the money into a Section 32 annuity. However, regulations under the Social Security Act 1986 and the introduction of personal pension plans from 1 July 1988 will ease the situation considerably, as the following options will be permitted:

- to transfer monies between occupational schemes and personal pension plans,
- to transfer *from* retirement annuities *to* personal pension plans, and *to* occupational schemes,
- if the contract allows, to transfer monies from a Section 32 annuity into a personal pension plan or occupational scheme.

It will not be possible to transfer money into retirement annuities except from other retirement annuities.

Joining a new employer

With the problems outlined above, in particular the transfer value which you might be offered on leaving an occupational pension scheme, you may prefer to take out a personal pension plan which is fully portable. If you leave one employer and join another you can ask him to contribute to your personal pension plan. In fact, you might not even be eligible to join his scheme until you have completed a waiting period, so if you do change jobs frequently the amount of pension which you may build up may be very limited and you would be better opting for a personal pension plan anyway.

11 Pension related mortgages

'The money is locked away'.

One of the rules about pensions is that in return for the tax advantages, you can't have the benefits until you retire. However, money paid into a pension need not be totally 'lost' in the meantime either to you or, if you are self-employed, to your business. There are many lenders who will lend money, using property or other assets as security, with the facility to repay the capital out of the tax-free lump sum available as part of your retirement benefits.

For many people these loan arrangements have provided the twin benefits of providing for the future and having cash available if they need it in the meantime.

'Pension mortgages' is an expression which often appears in newspaper and magazine articles about financial planning and various ways of borrowing money. In fact, there is no such thing as a 'pension mortgage'. It is not possible to borrow by mortgaging the pension. If you were to try to do this you would risk losing all the tax advantages of a pension scheme. Pension scheme rules will normally contain words such as '. . . your pension is non-assignable and may not be used as security for a loan . . .'.

Interest-only loan

The correct way of describing a loan which is connected in some way with a pension plan is 'an interest-only loan'. The lender, say a bank or building society, lends you money for a specified period during which you pay interest to the lender. At the end of the period the money (capital) has to be repaid. The lender will normally take security in the form of your personal assets, usually the house which you wish to buy. The lender will hold the deeds to the house, at the end of the period you will repay the loan, the deeds will be returned to you and you will own the property outright.

The alternative to an interest-only loan is the repayment loan where each payment consists of interest and capital. This is the 'traditional' building society mortgage.

With an interest-only loan a lender would normally wish to make sure that you have the means to repay the capital at the end of the period. If, for some reason you fail to accumulate the capital the lender can always realise his security (eg, by selling the house), but this is an action that most lenders would rather avoid taking.

Traditionally, you will have taken out an endowment assurance policy with an insurance company under which you will pay regular contributions. The policy will normally be assigned to the lender. At the end of the period the insurance company will pay the proceeds of the policy directly to the lender who will keep the capital that is owed, paying any balance to you. An endowment mortgage is an example of an 'interest-only' mortgage.

A pension-related mortgage

An interest-only loan which is arranged in connection with a pension plan operates on a basis which is very similar to an endowment mortgage. You pay interest to the lender during the term of the mortgage and repay the capital at the end of the term. But the money which you set aside each month to repay the capital does not go into an endowment assurance policy but into a pension plan. At the end of the term when you come to repay the capital you may use the tax-free lump sum to repay the debt.

When you actually come to repay the loan at the end of the term you can, of course, use any capital that you might have, eg, bank account, stocks and shares, building society accounts, not necessarily the tax-free cash available under your pension plan.

This is a useful point to bear in mind because your pension benefits could well be limited, especially in an occupational scheme. Consequently, although this is a tax efficient way of repaying your loan, you should regard it as a method to get you into your house in the first place. As your finances improve (and assuming you are paying the maximum you can into your pension), you should consider perhaps taking out an endowment assurance in addition, specifically to repay your mortgage so as to leave your pension benefits intact (although see later section on 'lifetime loans').

Endowment versus pension

If, under an endowment mortgage, you are required to invest £100 a month into an endowment assurance (in order to repay the mortgage at the end of the term) you would be no worse off if you were paying £133 a month into a pension (because, if you are a basic rate taxpayer you will obtain tax relief on the £133 resulting in a net cost to you of £100).

At the end of, say, 25 years the pension plan is bound to be much higher, not just because 33% more has been invested but because the pension plan will, in general, grow at a higher rate than an endowment assurance (for more information on this type of comparison see Chapter 7).

Consequently, you may be able to use your money more

effectively through a pension related mortgage with the one important proviso that you cannot get at your pension fund until you retire. With an endowment policy this restriction does not apply and if the investment growth has been higher than expected you may be able to pay off your mortgage early.

Obviously, if you are already contributing the maximum to a personal pension plan or if your employer is providing you with maximum benefits, you may be unable to pay additional contributions in which case you will have to use an endowment assurance.

Lenders' requirements

In the past where interest-only loans were arranged alongside a pension plan, the lender would normally require the borrower to have an individual pension plan, where benefits were ear-marked specifically for the member. With this type of plan it was easy to establish the value of the policy and the projected benefits which would emerge at retirement. By contrast, most lenders were **not** prepared to advance monies on an interest only basis where the borrower was in a group pension scheme, where the members' benefits were part of a common trust fund and not ear-marked specifically for a member.

Recently, however, lenders have been much more willing to ignore the differences between ear-marked policies and common trust funds and lend on an interest-only basis to members of group pension schemes. There is normally one requirement: that the borrower produces a statement, (which will have been prepared by the group scheme trustees), showing the benefits to which the member is entitled based on his service to date and prospective service to retirement, and in particular, an estimate of the tax-free lump sum which will be payable.

Lifetime loans

The most recent development in this field has been the facility to borrow on an interest-only basis where the capital is repaid out of the borrower's estate when he dies. In this case you do not have to repay the capital at the end of a period but the obligation continues with the loan until death. Thus, there is no need to use up any tax-free cash emerging from a pension scheme to repay a loan but there is, of course, a need to ensure that you have a sufficient income in retirement to enable you to continue to pay interest on the loan. Consequently, you should increase your pension contributions to build up the additional pension required. The lender will require you to take out a suitable whole life assurance policy assigned to the lender. Alternatively a term assurance policy may be accepted provided that it has an option allowing the policyholder to convert it into a whole life assurance.

(A whole life assurance is an insurance contract which pays out a sum assured in the event of your death at any time rather than one which pays out if you die within a specified period.)

A lifetime loan is a very useful option especially where the interest you are paying on your mortgage qualifies for tax relief (which is on mortgages of up to £30,000 taken out to buy or improve your own home).

If part of the loan is over the tax relief limit it is possible to repay that part on retirement, with the balance of the loan being repaid on death.

The lifetime loan option is a natural development in what has been a changing pensions environment in recent years, particularly in view of the restrictions on the amount of tax-free cash that may be taken from pension schemes (see Chapter 14) and the introduction of free-standing AVC schemes where only a pension may be provided and there is no facility to take a cash lump sum.

Personal pension plans

The introduction of personal pension plans from 1 July 1988 is likely to result in an upsurge in pension related loans. As explained in Chapter 4, personal pension plans which are used for contracting-out will receive contributions from the DHSS which will generate 'protected rights'. It is not possible to take any part of protected rights in the form of a tax-free lump sum.

However, the additional contributions that you may pay can generate a tax-free lump sum on retirement (see 'funding for cash with protected rights') and this cash lump sum could be used to repay a loan. Normally, cash-flow is of extreme importance when you are borrowing money and this method will enable you to borrow on the basis which requires the least outlay.

12 Approaching retirement

'Pensions can wait'.

To provide an income in retirement you need a lump sum of money. The more you save, the larger that lump sum of money is going to be and the bigger your retirement income. The later you leave it, the more difficult it is to build up that lump sum. With every passing birthday, it gets tougher to avoid the prospect of ending up poor after a lifetime's work.

Planning for retirement

However much you may have put off thinking about retirement and pension planning when you were young it is essential to review your likely retirement income as you get older. It is dangerous to plan for retirement at age 60 or 65. It is much more likely to come earlier, probably between 55 and 60. Planning should therefore start at around 40 to 45 at the latest.

Retirement planning should be part of your overall financial planning which you should carry out and review on a regular basis. If you are a member of an occupational scheme you will receive annual statements from the pension trustees showing your retirement income. Rather than just filing away the statement in a drawer you should consider whether the income is going to be adequate. If there is a short fall you will normally have plenty of scope of bridging the gap through free-standing AVC schemes.

If you are self-employed there will be no regular statement
from scheme trustees to jog your memory, perhaps only a
renewal notice from an insurance company suggesting that
you might top up your pension contributions to a retirement
annuity or personal pension plan. Once again, don't just file
these reminders away. If you start missing the opportunity to
keep your pension benefits in line with your rising income
you may never be able to catch up. Remember, your
contributions are **limited** so you may not be able to pay more
in the future.

Options in retirement

Regardless of how much you may have contributed to your
pension plan in the past, when you decide to take benefits
you will have to consider the options available to you which
will normally include the following:

- To take part of the benefits in a form of a tax-free lump
  sum.
- To decide whether you want a pension to be paid during
  your lifetime or a lower pension which will continue
  during the life of your surviving spouse.
- To choose a pension which will increase in payment.

The availability on these options depend on the type of
pension scheme. Under a retirement annuity contract or
personal pension plan you will have the above options. Under
an occupational scheme it is likely that a specific spouse's
pension is payable in the event of your death after retirement
so there is no need for you to give up part of your own
pension to provide for a spouse's pension. Also, in an
occupational scheme it is common for pensions to increase
in payment at say 3% or 4% per annum compound. Some
generous schemes, usually in the public sector, provide for
pensions to be increased in line with the cost of living.

Under individual schemes, such as retirement annuities and personal pension plans more flexibility is normally available. For example, if you had built up £100,000 in your pension fund at age 65 and you are a man you might have the following choices of annuity:

- An annuity of £14,000 a year payable during your lifetime annually in arrear ('in arrears' means waiting 12 months for the first payment).
- An annuity of £12,900 a year payable during your life monthly in advance ('in advance' means that payments start immediately).
- An annuity of £12,600 a year during your life payable monthly in advance but for a minimum of 5 years.
- An annuity of £10,500 a year payable during your life, monthly in advance for a minimum of 5 years increasing each year by 3% per annum compound.
- An annuity of £10,300 a year payable during the lives of you and your wife, assuming she is 3 years younger than you.

You do not have to decide on what type of annuity to take until retirement.

The above figures assume an underlying interest rate of 10%.

Open market options

Under retirement annuities and personal pension plans and also under occupational schemes providing ear-marked benefits for individuals, you will have an 'open market option'. This means that it is possible for the fund built up under the contract to be transferred to another insurance company which would then provide the annuity. You would exercise the open market option if you could obtain a higher annuity elsewhere. The annuity that you buy in this way is called a compulsory purchase annuity'.

A fund of £100,000 built up under a retirement annuity might provide an income payable in monthly instalments, throughout your life assuming you are a man aged 65, guaranteed for 5 years of £12,600 per annum but subject to tax at, say, 25% leaving a net income of £9,450 per annum.

Alternatively, the fund could be taken in the form of a tax-free lump sum of say £25,000 plus a reduced income of £9,470 (gross) netting down to £7,102: the cash of £25,000 could be used to buy purchased life annuity. When you buy a purchased life annuity, part of the annuity is regarded as a return of the purchase price – known as the capital content and is not taxed: the balance of the annuity is interest and is subject to tax.

The cash lump sum £25,000 could be used to provide a purchased life annuity of £3,060. Of this, £1,500 is interest and would be taxed (leaving a net income of £2,685 for a basic rate taxpayer).

The combination of the two annuities is therefore £9,787, an increase of £337 over the income obtained if the whole fund is used to buy compulsory purchase annuity.

Deferring your pension

If you have a retirement annuity or personal pension plan you have complete flexibility as to when you take the benefits. Under the former you can take them in stages between the ages of 60 and 75 and under the latter between ages 50 and 75. If you have income or capital outside of your pension fund you should consider using that to provide you with your retirement income and defer taking your benefits from your pension plan until the last possible moment. The reason for this is that your pension fund will usually be increasing at a higher rate than your non-pension fund investments because of the tax advantages of the former. For example, if you had built up a retirement fund of £100,000 by age 60 it would have accumulated to just over £200,000 by age 66, assuming that pension fund growth amounted to around 13% per annum. It is likely that similar non-pension fund investments would be growing at just under 10% per annum.

Life assurance in retirement

Normally, any life assurance benefit provided in connection with an occupational scheme or personal scheme will cease at a specified age – usually 60 or 65. The main function of life assurance benefits under occupational schemes is to provide benefits for your dependants if you die in the service of the employer. However, under personal pension plans and retirement annuities it is possible for life assurance benefits to be provided in the event of your death before age 75 regardless of whether or not you have retired.

In either case it is likely that you will wish to provide life assurance benefits for your dependants should you die after retirement. The need for life assurance does not disappear when you retire. Normally, the life assurance benefit which ceases when you reach pension age under an occupational scheme may be converted, regardless of your state of health, into an ordinary life assurance policy, provided you make the switch within a specified period (normally one month after you have retired from the company).

13 Pensions for directors

'My business will provide for my retirement'.

You may have successfully built up your own business which may be worth a substantial sum of money – today. But it is not for sale today. It is going to be for sale when you want to retire, when the pressure will be on you to sell it, not on the buyer to buy it. Although it is a success in today's business environment can you guarantee its continuing success for the next 20 or 30 years? What happens to your business (and your future) if you have an accident?

If your business is so successful today is this something you are prepared to gamble your future on, or should you be using its success to protect your future?

If you are a director of a private company (a family company as opposed to a public company) it is possible that you have never seen the need for a pension plan. You may well consider that your business is your pension and that, when you wish to stop working and retire, you will simply sell the business for a lump sum which can be invested to provide you with an income. Alternatively, you might consider that you will never retire and that you will pass the business on to your family. Indeed, it is possible that you inherited the business from previous generations. When you pass the business to your children hopefully they will be able to provide you with an income of some form.

Part of the problem, once again, is that few people relate to the idea of an 'old age pension'. You want to retire while you are young enough to enjoy it and you don't want a 'pension' – you want an income. Your real need is to have the option

to retire in comfort at a planned date in the future with no
financial worries.

In short, there is a need for future financial independence.

There is, of course, the State scheme but the modern trend
is to make us less dependent on the State, not more. In any
case, State pensions are geared at least to average earnings.
For the high-income earner, a large part of current income
is simply ignored as far as future income is concerned.
Nevertheless, for many people (even executives) pensions
are an uncomfortable subject, because of their connection
with old age.

All the key employees of a private company will be committed
to its profitability. This will bring financial rewards while
you are working and lay the basis for future financial rewards
when you stop working.

The problem is, providing these future rewards simply isn't
straightforward. Moving money from the company to
individuals to build up funds for retirement is complicated
by taxation:

- The company **could** pay higher salaries – but higher
  salaries merely attract higher taxes – making it difficult
  to accumulate capital.
- If the profits are paid out as dividends (to increase income)
  they are liable to income tax and do not save corporation
  tax.
- Profits could be accumulated within the company to build
  up the value of individual shareholdings – but these
  profits are liable to corporation tax and, in any event,
  income tax may still be payable by the individuals.
- A shareholding in the company is potentially liable to
  capital gains tax when it is sold, eg, to generate funds at
  retirement.
- Whatever happens there is always a potential liability to
  inheritance tax.

Overall, moving money from the company to the individual can mean that a proportion of the money will go to benefit the Inland Revenue. One way of avoiding corporation tax would be to make sure that all company profits are spent, but this of course would be unrealistic. Inevitably, some money will have to be retained in the business so that it is unlikely that corporation tax will be avoided completely.

In spite of all these taxation problems, you are still left with two main objectives when running your company:

- To run your business at a profit but at the same time keeping company and personal tax bills to a minimum.
- To make sure your hard work is rewarded in the form of the current and future financial well-being of both yourself and your colleagues.

Achieving these two objectives simultaneously looks difficult – but there is a straightforward solution.

The principal aim of your company, of course, is to make profits. It sells goods and services to generate an income and pays the expenses incurred in offering these goods and services to the public. The difference between the income and the costs is the profit – on which corporation tax becomes payable. It is here that every legitimate method will be used to reduce the amount of taxable profit and this is part of what is often meant by 'tax planning'.

An ideal solution, of course, would be to establish a *subsidiary* 'company' which did not suffer all the complications of taxation, and therefore made it possible for the directors and key employees to reap the rewards of their efforts and commitment to the company.

Fortunately, such subsidiary 'companies' already exist in the form of an executive pension plan.

Diagram 5

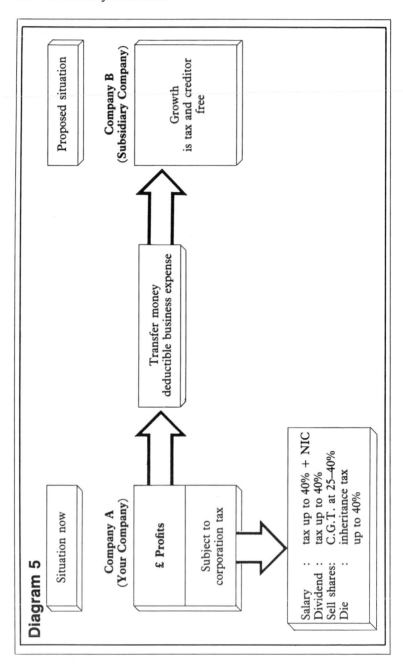

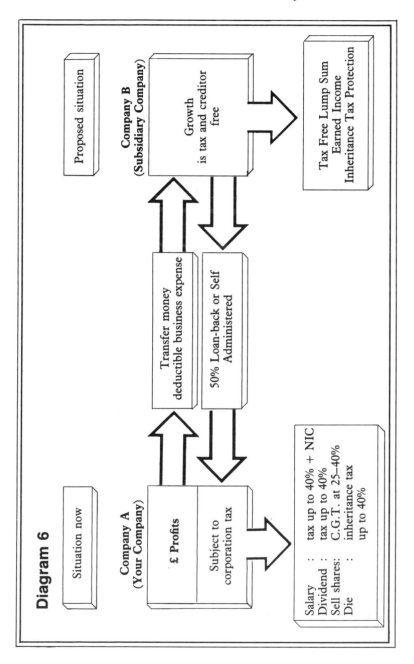

Diagram 6

Executive pension plans – tax advantages

An executive pension plan is the name often given to a pension plan which is set up specifically for directors or key executives of a company. Like any other occupational scheme it will be approved by the Inland Revenue under the Finance Act 1970.

The following tax advantages make it possible to build up a fund of money in order to provide for the future financial independence of the directors and key executives:

- All contributions made by the company to these retirement plans are allowable as a business expense and can be offset against taxable profits.
- Contributions made by the individual towards his own retirement fund are allowable against income tax at the individual's highest rates.
- All investment income and capital gains earned by the funds are free of all UK taxes.

In addition, the retirement fund built up for the future retirement benefits of key employees is protected against future financial misfortune as it is held in trust and does not form part of the assets of the company.

When the time comes to start taking the benefits of the retirement scheme, 3 other tax advantages come into play:

- A substantial lump sum (of up to £150,000) can be taken out of the fund totally tax free.
- The balance of the fund is used to provide a lifetime income which will be treated as **earned** income.
- The plan can have built-in life cover which can be paid direct to beneficiaries without incurring any liability to inheritance tax.

Overall, there can be few more successful ways of setting aside funds for the future than investing in this kind of retirement plan.

Full details on the types and levels of benefit which can be provided are set out in Chapter 14.

Personal pension plans or executive pension plans?

Either type of pension plan can be used if you are a director although in practice an executive pension plan will be more suitable as the benefits that may be provided are far greater. Under the personal pension plan the limits are on the contributions – generally 17½% of earnings whereas under an executive pension plan the limits are on the benefits that may be taken – as with any other occupational pension scheme. The limits are set out in in Chapter 14.

The following table shows the comparison of maximum annual contributions that may be invested as a percentage of current earnings:

Table 8

Age	Personal pension plan	Executive pension plan
25	17.5	84
35	17.5	94
45	17.5	117
55	20.0	261
57	22.5	401

Notes

1 It has been assumed that retirement age under the Executive Pension Plan will be 60, and that 20 years service will he completed with the employer by that date.
2 The above percentages are for men. In the case of women the percentages are the same for the personal pension plan but higher for the executive pension plan.
3 The percentages for the executive pension plan do not include the cost of providing death in service benefits.

The contracting-out decision

If you are a company director it is unlikely that you will wish to contract-out of SERPS as you will probably be paying substantial contributions into an executive pension plan (because of its use as a tax-planning device) to provide the maximum pension approvable by the Inland Revenue. Ideally, it is better not to contract-out of SERPS if there is any likelihood that you will be able to receive the maximum approvable pension. The reason for this is that on retirement you will be entitled to the maximum approvable pension plus the old age pension and SERPS so that your total entitlement will exceed two-thirds of your final remuneration. If on the other hand you contract-out the equivalent of SERPS must be provided within the executive pension plan so that overall your benefits will be limited.

Diagram 7 (page 107) demonstrates this point.

Loanback facilities

Subject to guidelines laid down by the Inland Revenue it may be possible for your company to borrow up to 50% of the monies invested in the pension plan from time to time provided that the loan is used for genuine commercial purposes. This means that your pension fund is another source of borrowing open to the company, alongside the usual sources of finance and your company can invest substantial contributions into an executive pension plan whilst retaining access to the funds. Loans can be considered for a number of business purposes such as the purchase, extension or modernisation of working accommodation, the purchase of capital items for use in business, and so on.

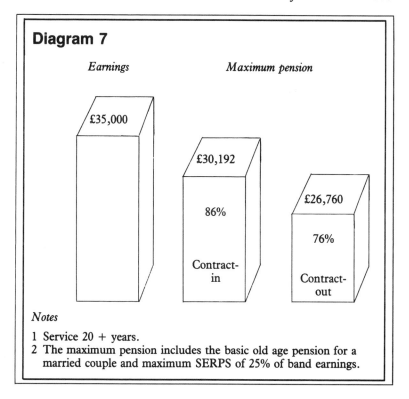

Diagram 7

Earnings   *Maximum pension*

£35,000

£30,192

86%

Contract-
in

£26,760

76%

Contract-
out

Notes

1 Service 20 + years.
2 The maximum pension includes the basic old age pension for a
  married couple and maximum SERPS of 25% of band earnings.

Small self-administered schemes

The maximum benefits that may be provided under a small
self-administered scheme are the same as under a
straightforward executive pension plan. However, whereas
under an executive pension plan the trustee has the power
to invest in an insurance policy, a self-administered scheme
gives the trustees wider powers of investment and these
include direct investment in stocks and shares, properties,
cash deposits, loans, etc. As with executive pension plans
offering a 50% loanback facility the trustees of a small self-
administered scheme may lend up to 50% of the assets back
to the company.

The Inland Revenue forbid the trustees from making any investments which might result in a personal benefit to the members of the scheme – usually the controlling directors of the company. For example, an investment in a residential property is unlikely to be acceptable to the Inland Revenue because of the possibility that this might be used by the directors themselves, or their families.

In practice, few directors do set up small self-administered schemes but you may be attracted to the notion of having control over the scheme's investment policy.

14 Inland Revenue limits

This chapter sets out the main limits applying under occupational schemes and executive pension plans if you become a member on or after 17 March 1987 (the date when various amendments were made to previous limits). Because these are limits laid down by law and because the law has changed so many times, they are a little complex in parts. If you need help in understanding them, you should talk to your financial adviser or write to your pension fund trustees.

Your normal retirement date

Your normal retirement date is the date at which you expect to retire and the date at which your benefits will normally become payable under your pension plan. Under an occupational pension scheme your normal retirement date is usually fixed by your employer and coincides with the date on which you will retire from the company, usually 60 for women and 65 for men. The choice could be important because if you wish to take benefits before your normal retirement date it will be treated by the Inland Revenue as early retirement and the maximum benefits allowed by the Inland Revenue may be restricted. The Inland Revenue will normally approve a normal retirement date within the range of 60 and 70 for men and 55 and 70 for women.

The Inland Revenue apply maximum limits to the benefits that you may receive under the plan. If you are entitled to (or have already received) retirement benefits from any employment or a retirement annuity plan, these limits may be lower. The limits are related to *service* and *final remuneration*.

The limits shown are those that normally apply to new scheme members. For members with 'reserved rights' (see below) these limits will, generally, be increased.

Service

Service means service from the date of joining your employer (not from the date when you join the scheme which is often later).

Final remuneration

'Final remuneration' means all earnings taxed under Schedule E (including fees, bonuses and benefits in kind but excluding the value of any share options or golden handshakes). For the purposes of calculating your pension benefits you may choose one of the following two definitions as an alternative to your actual salary in the year you retire:

- You may choose your basic salary paid in any one year out of the last 5 years before retirement, together with the value of any fluctuating income such as fees, bonuses and benefits in kind (although these may have to be averaged over a suitable period).
- You may choose 3 or more consecutive years ending in the last 10 years before retirement and calculate the average annual value of your total earnings, including fees, bonuses and benefits in kind.

If you are a controlling director (or if you have been one in the 10 years before your retirement), or if you have a final remuneration of £100,000 or more in 1987/88, or subsequently, you are **required** to use the second definition.

Any employee (excluding controlling directors) whose remuneration was £100,000 or more in 1986/87 will be able to use that highter figure and the first definition above if retiring within 5 years of 1986/87.

Lifetime income benefits

Provided you will have completed 20 years' continuous service with your present employer by normal retirement date or actual date of retirement, if later, then a maximum lifetime income of two-thirds of your final remuneration can be provided (though if you use part of the fund to take a cash lump sum, then your maximum lifetime income will be lower).

If your years of service are less than 20 the maximum pension is limited to 2/60ths of final remuneration for each year of service.

Tax-free lump sum

The scheme will always provide a basic tax-free cash lump sum of 3/80ths of your final remuneration for each year of service to normal retirement date although it may be possible for this amount to be increased to an upper limit of 1½ times your final remuneration.

The amount by which the basic cash entitlement may be increased is a percentage of the difference between 3/80ths of final remuneration and the maximum set out in the table shown below. The increase is related to the amount by which your **actual pension** entitlement exceeds a basic pension of 1/60th of your final remuneration for each year of service.

Table 8

Years of service to retirement age	Maximum cash sum as a percentage of final salary
1 to 8	3.75% for each year
9	37.50%
10	45.00%
11	52.50%
12	60.00%
13	67.50%
14	78.75%
15	90.00%
16	101.25%
17	112.50%
18	123.75%
19	135.00%
20 or more	150.00%

The following diagram explains how this works. In practice it is a complicated area and you should get advice if you want to know what your exact cash sum will be.

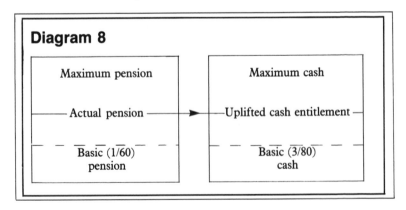

Diagram 8

Maximum pension	Maximum cash
── Actual pension ──►	──Uplifted cash entitlement ──
Basic (1/60) pension	Basic (3/80) cash

For example, say your pension under the scheme amounts to

35/60ths of your final remuneration (your employer having provided you with 1/60th of your final remuneration for each of your 30 years, service with the remaining 5/60ths having been purchased by your AVCs. Your basic cash entitlement will be 90/80ths (112.5%), ie, 3/80ths for each of your 30 years' service. However, because your total pension of 35/60ths exceeds the basic entitlement (30/60ths) by 16.67% your cash entitlement may be uplifted by the same percentage ie to 131%. Any such uplift must not take the cash entitlement above the maximum of 1½ times your final remuneration.

For the purposes of calculating the tax-free lump sum only, any final salary in excess of £100,000 will be disregarded resulting in a maximum cash lump sum of £150,000. This limit may be increased in future years, by Treasury Order, but it is not indexed and will not, therefore, automatically increase each year.

Widow's or widower's pension on death after retirement

If you choose a pension that will continue for your widow(er)'s lifetime after your death, then the maximum income that he or she may receive is two-thirds of your maximum lifetime income.

Death in service benefits

Lump sum benefits

The maximum lump sum death in service benefits which the trustees may pay is:

- A lump sum of 4 times your earnings at the date of death.
- If you have made any personal contributions to the scheme, then the relevant proportionate part of the fund will be returned as an additional lump sum.

The lump sum benefits can normally be paid free of all liability to inheritance tax.

Widow's or widower's pension

This is based on the number of years' service that you would have completed with your current employer if you had lived until your selected retirement age. If you could have completed 20 or more years' service then the maximum lifetime income payable to your widow/widower (or other dependant) would be 4/9ths of your earnings at the date of your death.

If your length of service would have been less than 20 years, the maximum lifetime income that your widow or widower may receive is two-thirds of your own maximum pension again based on your earnings at the date of your death.

Controlling directors

For controlling directors there are some modifications to the Inland Revenue limits.

Broadly speaking, you are a controlling director if you are a director and own or control (either directly or indirectly) shares carrying 20% or more of the voting rights in the company providing the executive pension plan or a company that controls that company. You have to include shares owned or controlled by your relatives and the trustees of any settlement in which you or your relatives have an interest. You do not need to own any shares yourself.

The most important modifications are that:

- Your final remuneration is not assessed as your earnings in the last year before retiring, but as your average total emoluments over any 3 or more consecutive years ending not more than 10 years before your retirement.
- If you die at the age of 75 or later, before actually retiring or taking your retirement benefits, lump sum benefits can only be payable to your widow or widower. If you do not leave a widow or widower, these benefits will be payable to your estate and will be liable to inheritance tax.

Reserved rights

Reserved rights allow an individual who was a member of a scheme prior to 17 March 1987 to retain the rights to benefits on the basis available before that date, which were generally higher than those explained above. This means that you will continue to benefit from 'pre-Budget 1987' rules whilst you remain in the same employment even if you subsequently join a new scheme of the same employer (eg, a new executive pension plan taken out to top up the benefits provided by a scheme of which you were a member before 17 March 1987).

15 Maximising tax relief in a personal pension plan

Chapter 3 looked at how a personal pension plan can be used to contract-out of SERPS and Chapter 4 considered the benefits that may be provided. This chapter looks at the contributions that you may pay and various ways of maximising tax relief. The methods outlined below apply to personal pension plans which you may take out from 1 July 1988 and also to retirement annuities which you may take out before that time. In the future it will be possible to have both types of plan running concurrently although you will not be able to take out a new retirement annuity after 30 June 1988.

Maximum contributions

The maximum contributions that you may pay (with effect from 6 April 1987) to a retirement annuity depends on your age at the beginning of a tax year and are expressed as a percentage of your 'net relevant earnings', ie, your gross earnings if you are an employee or, if you are self employed, your gross profits after deductible business expenses. For the tax year 1987/88 the percentages are as follows:

Age	Maximum contribution
Up to 50	17.5%
51 to 55	20.0%
56 to 60	22.5%
61 or more	27.5%

These percentages will also apply to personal pension plans, available from 1 July 1988. However, the above percentages are the overall contribution benefits to be applied if you are contributing to both a retirement annuity and personal pension plan.

The percentages also include any contributions which you may pay for life cover, ie, 5% of your net relevant earnings.

The maximum contributions relating to earlier tax years are based on your year of birth. The following table shows contributions from 1980/81 onwards:

Table 9

Year of birth	1980/81 to 1981/82	1982/83 to 1986/87
1934 or later	17.5%	17.5%
1916 to 1933	17.5%	20.0%
1914 to 1915	20.5%	21.0%
1912 to 1913	23.5%	24.0%

The above table is important because it is possible to pay contributions not only for the current tax year but also for previous years if you have not paid contributions in the past.

Carry back of contributions

It is possible for you to pay a contribution and choose to have it treated by the Inland Revenue as having been paid in the previous tax year. This might be particularly useful if your tax rates were higher in the previous year than in the current year. Also, by carrying back you should be able to obtain a refund of tax paid whereas if the contribution is relieved against your current earnings, you will normally obtain relief throughout the remainder of the tax year by having your tax coding adjusted (if you are an employed person).

If you are self-employed and you pay a contribution during the tax year 1988/89 and relief is claimed against that year, this will reduce the tax bill which will be due in January 1989 and July 1989. However, if the contribution is carried back to the tax year 1987/88, the tax was due in January 1988 and July 1988. If, therefore, the contributions are paid after July (assuming that you are up to date with your tax payments), a refund can be obtained from the Inland Revenue. If you pay the contribution in time before the July payment the contribution will reduce the July payment and you will obtain virtually immediate tax relief.

Obviously, if by carrying back you would obtain tax relief at, say, 27% (the basic rate of tax in 1987/88) but if you were to claim the relief against the year of payment to give relief at, say, 40% it would be advisable not to carry back. This sort of situation may arise if your profits, in the case of a self-employed person, or your earnings in the case of an employed person, suddenly start to take off, or are boosted by a special one-off increase in income.

Carry forward of contributions

As well as paying a contribution for the current year, or carrying back to the immediately previous year, you may also pay contributions in respect of years before that, using the percentages applying in those years, as set out in Table 9. If you wish to make up these missed contributions, you must first pay the maximum allowable contribution related to your net relevant earnings in either the current tax year or, if you are carrying back, the previous tax year.

You can make up for these missed contributions over a 6 year period, beginning with the earliest year. To take an example, if you wish to pay a contribution to be relieved against the tax year 1988/89 the contribution will be treated as representing first the appropriate percentage, say 17.5% of net relevant earnings for 1988/89 then a payment in respect of missed contributions for the tax years 1982/83, 1983/84 and so on.

Combination of carry back and carry forward

If you wish to pay a contribution and carry it back to the previous year you can also make up for missed contributions **6 years back from the year against which relief is to be claimed**. To take an example, if you pay a contribution during the 1988/89 tax year and carry it back to the tax year 1987/88 the contribution will be treated as representing the appropriate percentage, say, 17.5%, of net relevant earnings for 1987/88 then a payment for missed contributions from the tax year 1981/82, 1982/83 onwards.

It is important to remember that although the amount of missed contributions is calculated according to the percentages which applied in previous years, relief is granted against the tax bill for the tax year in which the contribution is paid, or a preceding year if the contributions are carried back.

If, for example, you paid 60% tax in 1984/85 and 25% tax in 1988/89, and you did not pay any contributions to a retirement annuity or a personal pension plan in the past and wish to start doing so now you may pay a contribution of, say, 17.5% of your earnings for 1988/89 plus 17.5% of your earnings in 1984/85 (when you were paying tax at the higher rate), but the total contribution will be relieved at only 25%.

Over-contributing

In order to achieve effective relief you must have sufficient taxable earnings against which to offset your contributions. If you have relevant earnings of £8,000 and your personal allowances are, say, £3,400 assuming you have no other income you will pay tax on £4,600. You might be able to pay contributions to a retirement annuity or a personal pension scheme, including missed contributions from previous years of, say, £5,000. However, you will obtain tax relief on only £4,600, which is the amount of relevant earnings which would otherwise bear tax.

This is an example of where the proposed contribution of £5,000 should be split, if possible, so that part of the contribution is carried back to the previous year with the balance being claimed against the current year.

If you pay no tax then you will not receive any relief. For this reason you should not over-contribute and in any case you might have been better off investing the 'over-contribution' in an alternative investment with the potential for similar growth but which does not have the same restrictions as to when you can take your benefits.

Mechanics of carry back

In order to carry back a contribution to the previous tax year, the following procedures must be followed:

1 The contribution must be received by your pension provider by 5 April in the year of payment.

2 An election must be made in writing to the Inspector of

Taxes by 5 July following the end of the tax year in question.

In the case of retirement annuity contributions there is an earlier 5 April deadline but the Inland Revenue do have a discretion to accept elections up to 5 July. In the case of personal pensions the individual has the right to delay the election until 5 July. **The contribution will still have had to have been paid by the previous 5 April.**

3 The contract must have been issued by 5 April.

4 An election for carry back may be made in the middle of a tax year. Normally, the Inland Revenue treat all methods of payment (annual, monthly or single) alike for tax relief purposes. However, in the case of such a 'mid-year election' the Inspector of Taxes will generally agree to carry back only contributions actually paid (ie, will exclude monthly payments due later in the year).

It is important to realise that the Inland Revenue adhere very strictly to these rules and will make no exception, for whatever reason, except where they are entitled to exercise their discretion as mentioned in 2 above.

Examples of carry forward/carry back

The following examples demonstrate how the carry forward and carry back facilities may be used together to provide an ideal solution depending upon your circumstances.

EXAMPLE 1: (Steadily increasing income)

Shows the position where income has been rising steadily and suggests that in such cases you should carry back as much contribution as possible to the previous tax year.

Tax year	NRE	Maximum percentage	Maximum contributions	Maximum unused relief	Taxable earnings	Tax rate
81/82	£ 6,000	17.5%	£1,050			
82/83	£ 8,000	17.5%	£1,400			
83/84	£10,000	17.5%	£1,750			
84/85	£12,000	17.5%	£2,100			
85/86	£15,000	17.5%	£2,625			
86/87	£15,000	17.5%	£2,625			
87/88	£20,000	17.5%	£3,500	£11,550	£14,000	27%
88/89	£21,000	17.5%	£3,675	£14,000*	£14,000	25%

*If carry back to 87/88 not used.

Question 1 What is the maximum contribution that may be carried back to 87/88?

Answer 1 £3,500 + £11,550 = £15,050. However, the contribution should be limited to taxable earnings, ie, £14,000.

Question 2 What is the maximum contribution allowable for the year 88/89 (assuming none of the contribution is carried back to 87/88)?

Answer 2 £3,675 + £14,000 = £17,675. However, the contribution should be limited to taxable earnings, ie, £14,000. Note: 81/82 falls out of the calculation.

Question 3 How would tax relief be maximised?

Answer 3 £14,000 carried back to 87/88 less 27% tax relief = £10,220 net +£4,725 in 88/89 less 25% tax relief = £3,543, ie, £18,725 invested with net cost of £13,763.

Notes

1 The payment of £14,000 carried back to 87/88 'uses up' £3,500 for 87/88, all unused relief for the years 81/82 to 85/86 inclusive (a further £8,925) and £1,575 from the year 86/87. Thus £1,050 (ie £2,625 – £1,575) remains unused for the year 86/87 and is carried forward for use in 88/89.
2 The payment of £4,725 in 87/88 is thus the 88/89 maximum ie £3,675 plus the £1,050 unused relief from 86/87.
3 Unused relief from 81/82 to 88/89 inclusive is thus fully used up.

EXAMPLE 2: (Low income in current year)

Shows the position where your income has dropped dramatically in the current year (for example because of retirement) and demonstrates that it is essential to take advantage of the carry back facility as very little tax relief would be available in the current year.

Tax Year	NRE	Maximum percentage	Maximum contribution	Maximum unused relief	Taxable earnings	Tax rate
81/82	£ 6,000	17.5%	£1,050			
82/83	£ 8,000	17.5%	£1,400			
83/84	£10,000	17.5%	£1,750			
84/85	£12,000	17.5%	£2,100			
85/86	£15,000	17.5%	£2,625			
86/87	£15,000	17.5%	£2,625			
87/88	£20,000	17.5%	£3,500	£11,550	£14,000	27%
88/89	£ 5,000	17.5%	£ 875	£14,000*	£ 500	25%

*If carry back to 87/88 not used.

Question 1   What is the maximum contribution that may be carried back to 87/88?

Answer 1   £3,500 + £11,550 = £15,050. However, the contribution should be limited to taxable earnings, ie, £14,000.

Question 2   What is the maximum contribution allowable for the year 88/89 (assuming none of the contribution is carried back to 87/88)?

Answer 2   £875 + £14,000 = £14,875. However, the contribution should be limited to taxable earnings, ie, £500. Note: 81/82 falls out of the calculation.

Question 3   How would tax relief be maximised?
Answer 3   £14,000 carried back to 87/88 less 27% tax relief = £10,220 net + £500 in 88/89 less 25% tax relief= £375 net, ie, <u>£14,500</u> invested with net cost of <u>£10,595</u>.

Notes

1 The payment of £14,000 carried back to 87/88 'uses up' £3,500 for 87/88, all unused relief for 81/82 to 85/86 inclusive (a further £8,775) and £1,575 from the year 86/87. Thus £1,050 (ie £2,625 – £1, 575) remains unused for the year 86/87 and is carried forward for use in 88/89.
2 The payment of £500 in 88/89 leaves a further £375 for 88/89 to be carried forward.

EXAMPLE 3: (Low income in previous financial year)

Shows the position where your income has risen steadily but with one poor year (the previous financial year) and shows that very little, if any, of the contribution should be carried back.

Tax year	NRE	Maximum percentage	Maximum contribution	Maximum unused relief	Taxable earnings	Tax rate
81/82	£ 6,000	17.5%	£1,050			
82/83	£ 8,000	17.5%	£1,400			
83/84	£10,000	17.5%	£1,750			
84/85	£12,000	17.5%	£2,100			
85/86	£15,000	17.5%	£2,625			
86/87	£15,000	17.5%	£2,625			
87/88	£ 5,000	17.5%	£ 875	£11,550	£ 1,000	27%
88/89	£25,000	17.5%	£4,375	£11,375★	£18,900	25%

★If carry back to 87/88 not used.

88/89   Income tax bands 25%   0 – £19,300
                           40%   over £19,300

Question 1   What is the maximum contribution that may be carried back to 87/88?
Answer 1   £875 + £11,550 = £12,425. However, the contribution should be limited to taxable earnings, ie, £1,000.

Question 2   What is the maximum contribution allowable for the year 88/89 (assuming none of the contribution is carried back to 87/88)?
Answer 2   £4,375 + £11,375 = £15,750 which is less than taxable earnings. Note: 81/82 falls out of the calculation.

Question 3   How would tax relief be maximised?
Answer 3   £1,000 carried back to 87/88 less 27% tax relief = £730 net +£14,875 in 88/89:
£100 less 40% tax relief = £60 net
£14,775 less 25% tax relief = £11,081 net, ie, £15,875 invested at total net cost of £11,141.

Notes

1 The payment of £1,000 carried back to 87/88 'uses up' £875 for 87/88 plus £125 from 80/81.
2 The payment of £14,875 for 88/89 will be 88/89 maximum ie £4,375 plus unused relief from 82/83 to 87/88 inclusive (which is £11,375 less the £875 already used in respect of 87/88). The maximum contribution is thus £4,375 + £11,375 – £875 = £14,875.
3 The balance of the 81/82 year, ie, £1,050 – £125 = £925 is more than six years prior to 88/89 and cannot therefore be carried forward to 88/89, and hence is lost. Unused relief from 81/82 to 88/89 inclusive is thus fully used up apart from the £925 from 81/82 which has been lost.

16 What does that mean?

Pension schemes sometimes seem complicated because of the jargon that is used. The following is a list of the words and expressions often used by pension practitioners:

Accrual rate

The fraction of earnings for each year of service which forms the basis of pension entitlement in a final salary or average salary scheme. For example, '1/60th' for each year of pensionable service.

Accrued benefits

The benefits in respect of service up to a specific date calculated in relation to current earnings or projected final earnings. Sometimes known as accrued rights.

Added years

This is a method of increasing a member's benefits where additional periods of pensionable service are provided, especially when a transfer payment has been made from a previous scheme. Sometimes members have the option of paying additional voluntary contributions in order to purchase added years, for example, purchasing an additional 3 years' service can provide an extra 3/60ths of final remuneration (see Accrual rate.)

Additional Voluntary Contributions

Contributions, (AVCs), over and above a member's normal contributions (if any), which a member may pay in order to secure additional benefits.

Continuation option

Where a member leaves a pension scheme which also provided life assurance benefits, the insurance company underwriting those benefits will often give him the facility of continuing his cover under a life assurance policy, without having to provide evidence of health. There is normally a time limit of one month after leaving the scheme for the facility to be taken up.

COMP

The abbreviation for a Contracted which is Out Money Purchase Scheme available to employers from 6 April 1988.

Compulsory purchase annuity

When you come to take your benefits at retirement the trustees of your pension plan will normally pay a portion of the fund in the form of a tax-free lump sum. The balance of the fund must be used to buy an annuity for you up to Inland Revenue limits: this annuity is called 'compulsory purchase annuity'. (See Purchased life annuity).

Contracting-out

Electing to give up your benefits under the State scheme in return for paying reduced national insurance contributions. To contract-out you need to be a member of a contracted-out scheme or contracted-out personal pension plan.

Contracted-out scheme

Where an occupational or personal pension scheme is used to provide its members with a level of benefits replacing part of the benefits from the state earnings related scheme that they would have enjoyed had they not been members of a contracted-out scheme.

Deposit administration

A type of insurance policy where contributions, after expense charges, are accumulated and to which interest and/or bonuses are added. The interest usually reflects prevailing interest rates or building society lending rates.

Executive pension plan

A pension scheme for directors of private companies or key executives.

Free-standing AVCs

An additional contribution, by a member of an occupational scheme, to another scheme which is completely separate. The total of the individual's contributions to both schemes is limited to 15% of remuneration.

Joint notice

A document which is completed by an individual and a pension provider and sent to the DHSS stating that the personal pension scheme entered into by the individual is to be used for contracting-out of SERPS and requesting the DHSS to remit the minimum contribution to it.

Lower earnings limit

The minimum amount which must be earned before national insurance contributions become payable to the state scheme. Once the limit is exceeded, contributions are payable in respect of earnings both above and below the limit. The level is approximately the same as the basic single person's pension. (See Upper earnings limit).

Net relevant earnings

If you are self-employed your profits from your trade, profession or vocation less deductible business expenses. If you are employed, your gross earnings.

Paid-up benefit

A preserved benefit secured for an individual member under an insurance policy where premiums have ceased to be paid in respect of that member.

Pensionable earnings

The earnings on which benefits and/or contributions are calculated. Pensionable earnings may differ from actual remuneration in that they may exclude various items such as bonuses, overtime, commission and director's fees.

Pensioneer trustee

An individual widely involved with pension schemes and required by the Inland Revenue to be a trustee of a small self administered scheme.

Purchased life annuity

An annuity is purchased with your own money, rather than pension fund money. The tax-free cash which you receive from a pension fund is your money and you might use it to buy a purchased life annuity where only a portion of the annuity is subject to income tax.

Retained benefits

Retirement or death benefits in respect of an employee's earlier service with a former employer or an earlier period of self-employment.

Salary sacrifice

An agreement, normally in the form of an exchange of letters between an employer and an employee where the employee gives up part of his salary. The employer is then able to make a corresponding increase in his contribution to the pension scheme.

Top hat scheme

An alternative term for the executive pension plan.

Transfer payment

A payment made from one pension scheme to the trustees or administrator's of another when a member leaves the old scheme to enable the receiving pension scheme to give additional benefits.

Upper earnings limit

The upper amount of earnings (approximately seven times the lower earnings limit) on which an employee's national insurance contributions are payable to the state scheme.

Vested rights

The benefits under the scheme to which a member is unconditionally entitled if he were to leave service including related benefits for dependants.

Waiting period

Period of service which an employee may have to serve before being entitled to join a pension scheme.

Index

133

Other titles in this series:

Forthcoming titles include: